MAKING
TEDDY BEARS
To Treasure

MAKING
TEDDY BEARS
To Treasure

Brian & Donna Gibbs

David & Charles

A DAVID & CHARLES BOOK

Photography by David Johnson and Jon & Barbara Stewart
Book design by Kit Johnson

First published in the UK in 2001

A catalogue record for this book is available from the British Library.

ISBN 0 7153 1129 8

Printed in China by Leefung Asco
for David & Charles
Brunel House · Newton Abbot · Devon

CONTENTS

INTRODUCTION

Ever since the first teddy bears were made at the beginning of the twentieth century children have wanted to have their own bear to cuddle. Parents and grandparents have always enjoyed making toys for the children in the family. This book has been written to enable anyone, regardless of their sewing experience, to make a teddy bear for themselves or their children, which will last a lifetime and become something to treasure.

You will find a wide range of exciting styles and patterns to choose from in this book. Teddy Edward Bear, for example, is a fully jointed traditional teddy bear in the style of 1950s and 1960s bears. If you want a more fun design, try Baby Ellie who can suck her thumb and Barney, a huge sitting bear that teddy lovers of any age will fall in love with. Also included are partially jointed designs such as Jolly (shown opposite), whose enormous body demands to be cuddled all night long, and the sleeping bear that has no jointed parts at all.

The comprehensive instructions take both the beginner and more experienced bear-maker through every stage of making a fully jointed bear with the aid of clear step-by-step photographs. The design differences that make each bear unique are explained with step-by-step photographs in the relevant chapter.

Teddy bears have always been intended for young children to play with. However, by today's standards the first bears were rather dangerous. They had glass eyes that could splinter into sharp pieces and metal spikes in their joints. Happily, modern advances in technology and an awareness of safety issues has meant that we can now enjoy making teddy bears with approved safety components and materials, knowing that they will not harm children in any way.

We have explained all the skills and safety considerations you need to know, so that you can be sure you are creating a safe and suitable toy for children. Finally, there is a suppliers list at the back of the book so that you can obtain all the necessary materials, components and tools to make your bear.

MAKING THE BEARS

In this chapter we take you through the process of making your own teddy bear from cutting out your fur fabric to grooming your assembled bear. Both beginners and experienced bear-makers alike will find this illustrated step-by-step guide useful. First, we look at the tools and materials you will need.

MATERIALS AND COMPONENTS

Making soft toys at home has always been a rewarding hobby. The vast range of fabrics and other bear-making materials available today makes it a positive delight. With everything from inexpensive synthetic fabrics to natural materials such as mohair or alpaca available in so many different pile lengths and colours, you should be able to find the right fabric to make a bear for any age, occasion or colour scheme.

SAFETY ISSUES

There is a large following among collectors for traditional-style teddy bears, so you are likely to come across items that are intended for collector's or artist's bears. These replicate as accurately as possible original, old-fashioned teddy bears and use components that are not suitable for young children's toys. They are likely to be wooden joints fixed with metal pins, glass or boot button eyes that have to be sewn onto the head and are much easier for a child to pull out; wood-wool filling which will not conform to any of the strict safety standards.

When buying supplies it is a good idea to state that you require safety components. Any reputable supplier, when requested, will provide you with written confirmation of the various standards met by the materials and components that they supply.

Have safety uppermost in your mind even before you begin sewing toys by keeping small components away from little hands and picking up any dropped items straight away. Make sure, too, that you use safety components in the proper way when you are constructing your bear.

Safety issues are mainly common sense. When you have finished your project take a good look to make sure nothing potentially harmful such as a forgotten pin has been left behind, or you have added an unsuitable decoration. Remove any additions such as a ribbon around the neck if you are giving the toy to a very young child or baby. A good test is to see whether after fitting such items, you yourself can remove it. Then you will know that the child will have a safe toy to play with.

Natural fabrics

The very first teddy bears were made from mohair, a fabric derived from the fleece of the Angora goat, for the realistic look that could be achieved. Fabrics made from natural fibres are also hard wearing and they remain popular with teddy bear manufacturers and home toy-makers today. Mohair is available in many different pile lengths, qualities and colours from natural golds and browns to the vibrant reds and blues used to make Harley bear on page 29.

The quality of the fabric does not relate to whether it is of a good or poor standard but describes the finish given to the pile in the manufacturing process, which creates a texture on the material. Distressed mohair, for example, is 'permed' to make the pile lie in different directions. This will make your finished bear look well cuddled. Other fabric qualities you will come across include wavy, curly, embossed and sparse. Sparse mohair has much less pile woven on to each square inch of cotton backing than other types. This also gives the impression of an old, worn-out bear as the backing fabric is visible through the pile.

All qualities are available in a wide range of pile lengths from a very short 5mm to over 50mm. The short-pile fabrics are suitable for making small teddies while the longer lengths can make a large design like Barney look extra special. Although mohair is one of the most expensive plush fabrics especially if you choose a long pile, it can be quite economical when compared to high-quality synthetic fabrics.

Alpaca is a very similar material to mohair. The fibre for this fabric is obtained from the Llama instead of the Angora goat. It is available from specialist suppliers in a more limited range of colours and qualities (see Suppliers on page 125).

Synthetic fabrics

If you think there are lots of natural fabrics to choose from, just take a look at what is made from synthetic fibres. There's everything from pastel stripes to Friesian cow prints, in a bewildering range of colours, pile types and qualities. Some are of an inferior grade to natural fabrics while others are more expensive.

There are a few pointers to consider when buying this type of fabric. As with all materials, they come in different qualities. The cheapest end of the range has a knitted or jersey backing. This means that if you stuff your teddy firmly, the backing may stretch out of shape, spoiling the appearance of the finished toy. This type of cheap material is best used for softly-stuffed toys that are not expected to last for ever.

The middle range synthetic fabrics have a much higher finish, although they still have a knitted backing. This is much firmer and will only stretch a little. At the top of the range are the very dense pile fabrics. These are quite luxurious with the added feature of a woven backing and can be used in the same way as mohair. There is a down side, however, as this quality is not very common and is often more expensive than mohair.

Natural and synthetic fabrics are very different in appearance, and each one has its own strengths and weaknesses. High-quality synthetic materials can be much denser than natural fabrics, with a wonderful softness to the pile that mohair cannot match. On the other hand, mohair is incredibly hard wearing and versatile so you can try many alternative techniques with it, including dyeing the pile to suit your own needs.

Pad materials

Various materials are suitable for foot and paw pads, but felt and ultra-suede are the most popular ones. Felt was traditionally used for many years. Look out for a good-quality felt, ideally with a wool mix for durability and strength. You can buy 100% wool felt that is much thicker and stronger than ordinary craft felt, however, it can cost as much as mohair when bought by the metre.

Ultra-suede is fast growing in popularity as an alternative to felt. This is a man-made fabric that looks like natural suede and is wonderfully thin, yet still very strong. It does not fray and is as easy to sew as cotton fabric. It is available in a good range of colours.

Joints

Always use plastic safety joints when making teddy bears for children. These are widely available in all sizes, are easy to fit and very secure.

Each joint is made up of two plastic discs. One has a moulded shank and a one-way fixing washer made of metal or plastic. This cannot be removed without destroying the joint once it has been fitted, so it is essential to position it accurately first time. As these joints are made almost entirely of plastic, they are rust proof and will last the lifetime of your teddy bear or toy.

Eyes

Safety is also paramount for the eyes, and plastic safety eyes should always be used. Like the safety joints, these plastic eyes have a moulded shank. A one-way retaining washer is pushed over it to secure the eye in place.

These eyes are available in a wide range of sizes and colours from blues and greens to lilac. There are even solid black types that look like the antique boot button eyes fitted to early bears.

Noses

There are two ways of adding a nose to a teddy bear. One way is to embroider the nose in any size or shape using embroidery thread. An easier way is to use a plastic safety nose.

Like the safety eye, a safety nose has a moulded shank at the back that is secured with a one-way washer after it has been inserted through the fabric. These noses are moulded to look realistic and can be fitted as they are. However, they look even better covered with a fabric such as ultra-suede.

We used this technique to make Muzzwell Bear's nose on page 57. We also show you how you can improvise by using items in the home to make your own safety nose if you cannot buy one.

Filling

Polyester fibre is the most popular type of filling and the easiest to use. Happily, it is also the safest. It is available in different grades. The best grade is called hi-loft, which is both voluminous and soft, and is the best choice for stuffing toys. It is quite springy, retains its bulk, and does not form hard lumps when pushed into small areas. Check before buying that your filling conforms to the usual safety regulations, which the majority will.

At the other end of the range is coloured cotton waste. This conforms to safety standards, but is not really a suitable filling for soft toys as the finished result is likely to be rather lumpy.

Voices

A voice is a must when making a traditional-style teddy, but you can add one to any design. A voice or growler as it is also known, is a plastic cylinder into which is moulded a small bellows and reed. These growl when tipped first one way then the other to expel the air through the reed. They are available in different sizes. Voices can have a high failure rate, so you should always test them before buying. Listen to the growl carefully because some sound more like a cow or a sheep than a bear.

Another alternative is to use a musical movement. These are clockwork units that play a little tune and are set off by winding a key or by pulling a cord. Make sure that you buy a shelled unit. This means the working parts are encased in a plastic shell or box and will not let the stuffing come into contact with the mechanism. In other types the movement is exposed – these are only suitable for boxes.

Threads

Only a few types of thread are used to make teddy bears or soft toys. One is general sewing thread, often a polyester cotton mix, which is used for most of the stitching by machine. Next, strong thread or button thread as it is also known, is used to close the final seams where a secure and durable result is needed, and for stitching entire bears by hand.

Finally, you will need a thicker thread or embroidery silk if you are embroidering a nose or some claws. Wool is much too weak for this purpose and will also give the finished nose a fluffy look.

You will find that many threads have a manmade content to them and are labelled as 'mercerised'. This means the thread has been treated to make it slip through the fabric more easily, which is helpful when you are making toys and teddy bears.

TOOLS

Only a few tools are needed for making bears at home, but these should be of the highest quality.

Pattern-making materials

You will need tracing paper to transfer the patterns from the book and sturdy craft card to make them into working templates. Use a general-purpose ballpoint pen to trace the patterns and mark the cutting instructions on your templates.

You will also need a waterproof permanent marker pen with a fine tip that does not smudge, to mark your patterns on the back of the fabric. You can buy these from drawing supplies shops or most good stationers.

Scissors

Three types of scissors are required – general-purpose craft scissors, good-quality fabric scissors and embroidery scissors. Use the first set to cut out the paper patterns and card templates. Then you can keep your fabric scissors sharp enough for cutting the fur fabric. Finally, a small pair of embroidery scissors will prove invaluable for trimming mohair pile and cutting any loose threads.

Pins

To hold the pieces of fabric in position ready for sewing you will need some extra-long pins with large coloured heads. The extra length is necessary for holding the thick fabric securely, and you are more likely to see the coloured heads on any pins you have forgotten.

Needles

All of the designs in this book can be sewn by hand but you will probably prefer to use a sewing machine. Use a size 14–16 machine needle with a sharp or regular point on a woven-backed material and a ballpoint needle on a knitted or jersey-backed fabric.

If you are making your bear by hand, try a size 5–7 needle for oversewing the fabric pieces together and sewing the seams. However, this is a personal preference and you may find a different size needle more comfortable.

When closing final seams with strong thread, you will find it easier to use a longer or darning needle of around the same size. Use a thick darning needle the right size for your thread to embroider the nose on your bear if you are not using a plastic nose.

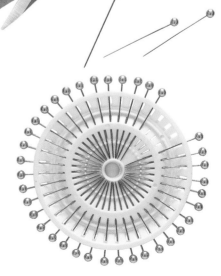

Thimble

It is a good idea to wear a thimble when sewing by hand, especially when working through multiple layers of thick fabric. This can be a metal capped one or for more versatility, consider using a leather thimble. This can be slipped onto your finger to help push the needle through the fabric, or it can be used on your little finger to pull on the extra-strong thread when closing seams. It will stop the thread from cutting into your skin.

Awl

You will need to make holes in the fabric for eyes and joints and a good awl is necessary for this. You can improvise by using the point of your small scissors, but be very careful as this method can often leave a much bigger hole than intended if the threads of the material are accidentally cut.

Safety tool

This neat little device is designed to help you push on the one-way washers on joints, eyes and noses. It is simply a flat metal plate with two different-sized holes that fit a wide range of assorted size components. Alternatively, you can use an empty cotton reel, but as these are now made from plastic they do tend to split.

Stuffing tools

It is possible to buy specially designed stuffing sticks with shaped handles that make them comfortable to use. However, these are quite expensive when you have ideal stuffing tools in your kitchen. The handle of a wooden spoon is ideal for stuffing larger bears, while a wooden or plastic chopstick with the point slightly removed will be perfect for small bears and intricate little crevices.

Teasel brush

Once your bear is stuffed and assembled, you will probably notice that some of the fur pile is trapped in the seams. To free this you can either use the point of a large pin or needle which will take a long time, or you can invest in a teasel brush.

These come in two basic designs, the most common being a little wooden block with metal bristles attached on one side. A more elaborate design has many more metal bristles as well as a handle, making it easier to use. This second brush is often sold in pet shops for grooming small pets.

A Guide to Making Bears

In this step-by-step guide we show all the stages involved in making teddy bears. Now all you have to do is choose which bear to make. You will find the bear patterns at the back of the book, from pages 77–124. Each pattern has a 7mm (¼in) seam allowance included. If you are sewing by hand, use extra-strong thread for secure seams. Use a medium stitch length on the sewing machine and sew each seam twice for strength. In bear-making it is best to pin and then oversew the seams together to anchor the fabric ready for stitching instead of using tacking (basting).

1 Making the templates

Trace all the pieces for your chosen bear from the templates on pages 77–124. Remember to include the reverse pattern pieces and to copy the pattern information. Paste the resulting paper patterns on to sturdy craft card. Cut out these card templates and make neat holes to indicate the joint positions.

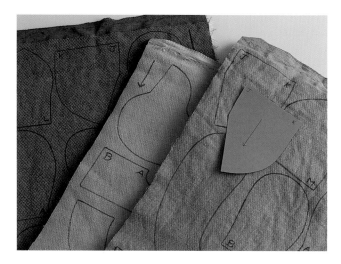

2 Marking the fabric

Now find the pile direction of your fur fabric by stroking it. It will feel smooth to the touch when you stroke it in the direction of the pile. Draw an arrow on the back of the fabric to show the pile direction. Lay the cardboard templates as close together as possible on the back of the fabric matching the arrows on the patterns to the one on the fabric. Draw round each piece with a marker pen, transferring the pattern information at the same time.

3 Cutting the fabric

Cut out the pieces using sharp fabric scissors. Using just the points, slide the scissors through the pile until the blade is touching the backing fabric. Make small, deliberate cuts following the outlines of the pattern until each piece is cut out. This will ensure you do not cut off the pile at the edges, which will show around the finished seams.

4 Making the head

Pin the head pieces right sides together from the nose, along the curved chin seam to the bottom edge. Oversew the pieces then stitch in place. Now insert the head gusset. Starting at the nose, pin one half of the head gusset to one of the head sides, ensuring that the back edges meet perfectly. Oversew this edge in position then repeat with the other side. When the head gusset is securely oversewn, stitch in place, leaving the bottom straight edges open.

5 Positioning the eyes

The positioning of the eyes will affect the expression on your finished bear. Loosely fill the head with polyester filling and use two felt circles the same size as the eyes to try out different expressions for your bear. Move these around until you are happy with the positioning, then pin them on.

6 Fitting safety eyes and noses

Remove the stuffing from the head and make a hole with the awl for each eye. Pass the shank of the eye through the hole and, from the inside of the head, secure the one-way washer firmly in place. Attach a plastic safety nose like the covered one used on Muzzwell Bear in the same way at the point where the seams meet on the front of the head.

7 Making a two-piece body

The designs in this book are made with either a two-piece or a four-piece body. On a simple two-piece body like Baby's First Bear on page 72 or the embroidered bears on page 41, first stitch any darts at the top and bottom of each piece. Then place the body pieces right sides together and stitch all round, leaving the gap marked on the pattern for turning.

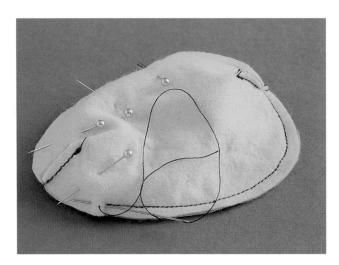

8 Making a four-piece body

On a four-piece body like Teddy Edward's on page 52, place one of the body fronts over the corresponding body back and stitch together along the side seam. Repeat with the other body front and back. Then join the two halves by placing them right sides together, pin and oversew the seam before stitching all round, leaving the opening for turning. Turn the right way out.

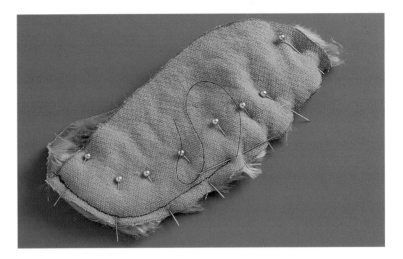

9 Making the arms

Cut out the paw pieces from ultra-suede or felt and place one on top of an inner arm piece with right sides together. Match the straight edge and pin in place. Oversew to secure then stitch. Open out this completed inner arm and place on top of an outer arm with right sides together. Pin and oversew in place then stitch leaving the opening marked for turning.

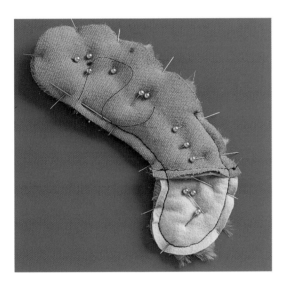

10 Making the legs

Place one leg piece on top of another with right sides together. Stitch around the leg leaving open the gap for turning and the bottom straight edge for inserting the footpad. Take one of the footpads and fold in half along its length to form a crease. This will help you position the footpad symmetrically. Starting at the toe, match the crease in the footpad to the seam at the front of the leg and pin to hold. Do the same at the heel of the foot, matching the crease to the back seam on the leg. Continue to pin around the footpad then oversew in place before stitching.

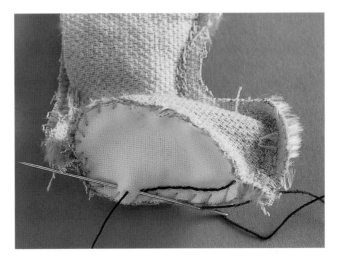

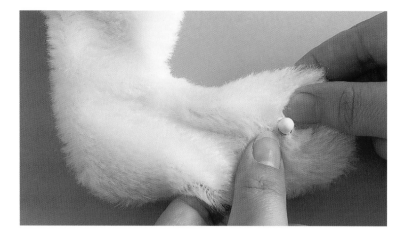

11 Inserting joints in limbs

Insert the joint in each limb before stuffing. Make a hole with the awl large enough for the shank of the joint to pass through at the point marked on the pattern. Take the part of the joint that has the moulded shank and place it inside the limb. Push the shank of the joint through the hole until it appears on the outside. The limbs can now be stuffed.

12 Stuffing

When stuffing a large bear, take a good handful of stuffing and push it into the bear. Use a chopstick or wooden spoon handle to push it into the area furthest away from the opening. Continue adding the stuffing, pushing it well in each time. Check that no hollow areas are created where filling is missing. If there are, you will have to take out some of the stuffing and start again. When the limbs are nearly full, add the filling in smaller amounts so that you can shape the bear as you go. This is especially important with the head. On a small bear, add smaller quantities of stuffing each time.

13 Inserting a joint in the head

The head must be stuffed firmly before its joint can be fitted. Take the stuffed head and invert it so that the open bottom edge is facing you. Lay the main half of the joint on the filling, with the shank pointing outwards. To enclose the joint in the head, thread a needle with strong thread and knot the end. Sew a running stitch all the way around the bottom edge of the head and pull tightly so that this edge is gathered around the joint, but leaving the shank protruding to the outside. Finish off the thread very securely.

14 Closing the seams with ladder stitch

Use ladder stitch to close the final seam of your jointed and stuffed limbs neatly. Thread a long needle with extra-strong thread and knot the end. Insert this into the fabric from the inside at the top of the opening so that the knot is anchored inside. Push the needle down into the fabric on the other side of the opening, and take a small stitch. Continue taking a small stitch before crossing over to the other side of the opening in this way until you reach the bottom. Pull the stitches tightly as you go (you may find a leather thimble useful). Leave your final stitch as a loop and pass your needle through it to form a knot. Take another small stitch on top of this knot and do the same again, then push the needle into the limb next to the knot and pull it out 5cm (2in) away. Pull the thread very tightly and cut it off level with the fabric. The thread end will retract inside the bear.

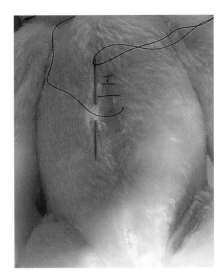

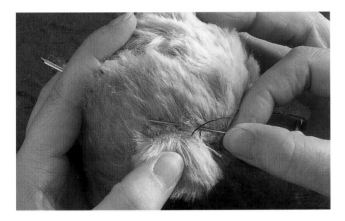

15 Making and attaching the ears

On a small bear you will need to sew these by hand. Place two ear pieces right sides together and stitch around the curved edge only, leaving the bottom straight edge open. Turn right sides out and close the bottom seam with ladder stitch. Pin the ears onto the stuffed and jointed head, trying out different positions until you find the right look. When you are happy with their position, use extra-strong thread to stitch them securely to the head with ladder stitch.

16 Preparing the nose

If you have not already added a plastic nose to your bear you will need to embroider one. Some of the patterns in this book include a nose template. Cut this out of felt in a shade to match your nose thread, trim the pile where the nose will go, and stick in place with all-purpose craft glue. You can then embroider over the top. On patterns that do not have this template, you can either make your own or embroider the nose without this aid. Either way the embroidery sequence is the same.

Make your bear look really special by embroidering the nose in a mixture of different coloured threads. Bracken Bear's nose includes a few strands of lilac cotton to match her beautiful fur

17 Embroidering the nose

Thread a needle with nose thread and secure the end invisibly by taking a few stitches into the bear's muzzle, each time inserting the needle into the hole it has just emerged from. Make a long straight stitch down the middle of the template extending below the bottom edge of it. Work a series of parallel straight stitches to cover the template moving from the central stitch to one edge of the template. Return to the central stitch and fill in the other side in the same way.

18 Adding the mouth

When you have covered the nose template, bring the needle out at one end of where you want the mouth to go, pass it under the long central stitch and take it back down directly opposite to form the mouth. Check that it is level before securing the thread in the same way as you began.

19 Assembling the bear

Find the marks on the inside of the body that indicate the joint positions. Attach the head to the body first because you will use it as a reference point when attaching the limbs. Using your awl, make a hole in the body large enough for the shank of the head joint to pass through. Pass the shank through the hole from the outside and fix on the one-way washer from the inside of the body, pushing it on as far as it will go. Do exactly the same with the limbs, checking first that they are the right way round. Then stuff the body and close the final seam with ladder stitch.

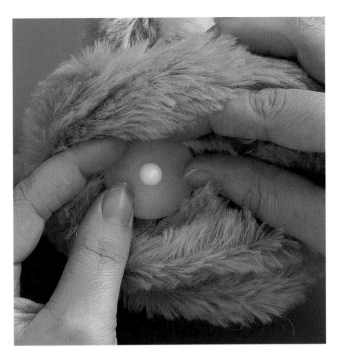

20 Grooming your finished bear

You may find some of the fur pile has become trapped in the seams, so give your completed bear a final grooming with a teasel brush to release it and make him look his best.

21 Adding a voice or musical movement

A voice or growler should be added between jointing and stuffing the body. Put a little stuffing in the front of the tummy area then fill the upper and lower parts of the body until a cavity just large enough to take the unit is left. Push the growler unit into the cavity horizontally with the holes facing forwards if you want the bear to growl when he is tipped backwards or the other way round if you want him to growl as he is tipped forwards. Add a small covering of filler to make sure it will not be felt from the outside. Insert a musical movement in the same way, except that the key must protrude through the opening when you close the final seam.

BARNEY BEAR

Everyone will want to have this magnificent large bear. Barney is designed with bent legs so he can sit on a shelf or chair and keep you company while you're busy around the house. He is made extra cuddly by using a long-pile mohair fabric and stuffing him softly. He also has unusually-shaped paws and feet. Barney will look just as handsome, if a little different, when made from a less expensive synthetic fur fabric.

you will need

- 60 x 137 cm (24 x 54 in), 25 mm (1 in) curly-pile mohair or synthetic fur fabric in beige
- 30 x 25 cm (12 x 10 in), felt or Ultra-suede for the paws and pads in beige
- Five, 65 mm (2½ in) plastic safety joints
- One pair, 16 mm (⅝ in) amber plastic safety eyes with black pupils
- 5 m (5½ yds), brown nose thread
- 1 kg (2.2 lb), polyester filling
- Sewing thread and strong thread to match

50 cm (20 in) standing

tip As well as being safer for children, plastic safety joints are handy when making a large bear like Barney. They are easier to secure in position than wooden joints.

1 Use the templates on pages 78–85 to cut out the pieces for Barney Bear as explained on pages 16–17. On a long-pile fabric like this, it is important to make sure that the pile runs in the correct direction on each piece. Take extra care over cutting out to ensure that you do not cut through the pile, which may spoil the look of your bear. See Marking the fabric on pages 16 for how to find and mark the pile direction, and Cutting the fabric on page 17.

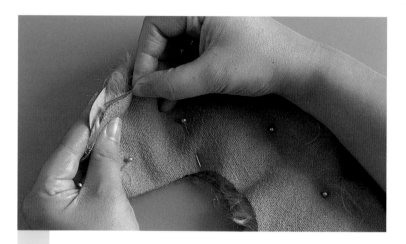

2 Make the head and body following the instructions on pages 17–19. Tuck the pile neatly to the inside when you are pinning the pieces together before oversewing them in place ready for stitching. This will help to make the seams less visible on the finished bear. Use a very strong thread if you are sewing by hand, or stitch each seam twice for extra strength on a sewing machine. Barney has a four-piece body.

3 Make the arms and legs as explained on page 19. Take extra care when stitching around the shaped ends. Your seams should follow the outline precisely to ensure that an even shape is achieved.

4 When making the legs, you will notice that the front of each foot pad is shaped but not the corresponding leg piece. You will need to trim a small amount from each leg piece to match the shape before it can be oversewn in position ready for stitching.

5 When you have sewn these pieces together, the bear is ready for jointing and stuffing (see page 20). From the inside of one of the limbs find the dot that indicates the joint position. Make a small hole with an awl and insert one half of the joint, pushing the shank through the hole you have made to the outside. Repeat on the other limbs.

tip Stuffing your bear loosely will give him a squashy, friendly feel. We used a high-quality polyester to stuff Barney's arms, legs and body loosely, taking care that the stuffing was evenly distributed. Barney's head, however, should be filled very firmly ready for embroidering the nose.

6 Stuff each limb and close the seam with ladder stitch (see page 21). Attach each one by making a small hole in the body where marked with an awl and pushing the protruding shank through the hole to the inside of the body. Place the other half of the joint over the shank and secure it with the washer.

7 Fill the head very firmly, especially at the muzzle, to give a good base for embroidering the nose. Attach a felt nose template if preferred (see Preparing the nose on page 21). Start by making the long central stitch as explained in Embroidering the nose on page 22. Then work a series of straight stitches first on one side of the central stitch, then on the other, until you have completely covered the nose template. Working the stitches in this sequence instead of completely covering one half of the nose before moving to the other side, will help to keep the nose straight and the tension even on a large nose like this.

8 Barney's feet are finished off by adding embroidered claws. These are very easy to work and can be added to any teddy bear design. Secure the end of the nose thread as if for embroidering the nose (see page 22), then bring the needle out behind the foot pad in the position where you want the first claw to go. Insert the needle into the top of the foot to create the first claw and bring it out through the foot pad again to make the second claw. Continue working in this way until you have stitched as many claws as you need, then securely fasten off the thread. Stitch the claws on the bear's paw pads in the same way.

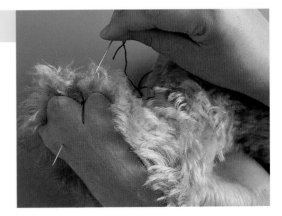

HARLEY THE CLOWN BEAR

Ever since teddy bears were first made, designers have looked for new ways to make their bears unique and thus more appealing. Clown bears were one such innovation. They were made from different coloured fabrics and often combined several colours on the one teddy. Harley Bear is designed in the style of one of these old bears. He is made from sparse mohair in muted colours which gives him a lovely worn and faded look.

you will need

- Three, 50 x 50cm (20 x 20in) pieces, 9mm sparse-pile mohair or synthetic fur fabric (one in each of these colours – pale gold for the head, feet and hands; a muted blue and dusty pink for the arms, legs and body)

- 20 x 15cm (8 x 6in), felt or Ultra-suede for the paws and pads in fawn

- Four, 35mm (1½in) plastic safety joints for the arms and legs

- One, 50mm (2in) plastic safety joint for the head

- One pair, 9mm black plastic safety eyes

- 2m (2yds), dull brown or grey nose thread

- About 450g (1lb), polyester filling

- Sewing thread and strong thread to match

For the hat and ruff

- 30 x 20cm (12 x 8in), craft card

- 30 x 20cm (12 x 8in), fawn felt

- All-purpose craft glue or hot-glue gun

- 10 x 5cm (4 x 2in), long-pile upholstery fabric (used for making miniature bears) or three, 2cm (¾in) pom-poms for the decoration

- 80cm (32in), 1.5cm (½in) wide double-faced satin ribbon for the hat ruff

- 150cm (59in), 3.5cm (1⅜in) wide double-fa
  neck ruff

38cm (15in) standing (without hat)

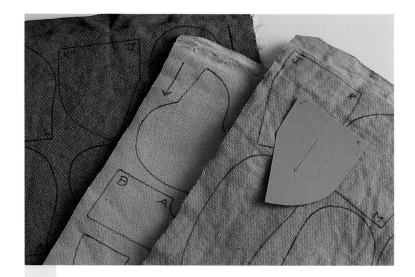

1 Use the patterns on pages 86–90 to make templates and cut out the pieces for Harley the Clown Bear as explained on pages 16–17. This bear is not difficult to make, but you should double check that you are cutting out and sewing together the correct coloured pieces. Mark each cardboard template with the cutting instructions (write them on the back for the reverse pieces), and add the reference letters to your fabric. Start by making the head (see page 17).

2 Place one pink upper body back and one blue lower body back right sides together matching points L and M. Stitch the two pieces together along this line to make a half body back. Join the two other body back pieces in the same way – this time the upper piece should be blue and the lower piece pink. Do the same with the body front pieces, matching the reference letters.

3 Stitch the two joined body front and two joined body back pieces together as explained in step 8 on page 19 matching the seams for a neater finish.

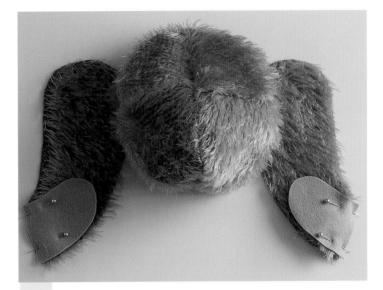

4 Hold the arm pieces up to the completed body to see which are the inner arms and which are the outer arms. Put the pink inner arm next to the blue front upper body and sew on the felt paw pads. Attach the gold hands to the outer arms and make one arm pink and the other blue as explained on page 19. Identify the leg pieces in the same way, but this time put the pink inner leg next to the blue front lower body. Join the upper and lower leg pieces from Points A to B before making a blue and a pink leg (see page 19).

5 Joint and stuff the pieces as explained on page 20. Close the seams with ladder stitch (see page 21). Either embroider your bear's nose as shown on page 22, or stitch a threadbare nose to make him look old and worn. This should look as if one of the nose threads has become unravelled so the stitching should be uneven. Secure the end of your nose thread and make a long central stitch. From this point work out towards the edges taking uneven stitches so that the backing fabric is visible between the stitches. See page 23 for how to assemble the bear.

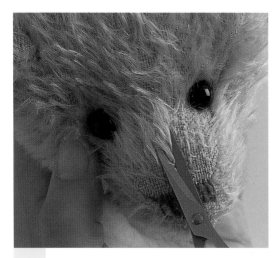

We also made a smaller and more contemporary version of Harley using bright-coloured fabric. To make your bear this size – 26cm (10in) – the patterns should be reduced to 70% of their original size. The nose is stitched in red embroidery thread and outlined in black. This bear has ruffles around his hands and feet as well as his neck, made in the same way as Harley's ruffles from 50cm (20in) lengths of ribbon.

6 You can also make your bear look older by trimming away the fur in areas where you would expect some wear. We limited this to the nose area but it can look just as effective when applied all over the body. Use a small pair of sharp embroidery scissors to gradually trim away areas of fur. Proceed slowly and carefully (you cannot stick the fur back on again if you trim too much). Check your progress frequently and stop when you have your desired look.

7 Harley's hat is a simple design made from felt-covered card. Use the template on page 88 to cut the hat piece from the card and also to cut a smaller piece of felt up to the dotted line. Using craft glue, stick the felt to the card matching the edges carefully. This will leave a small flap of card uncovered.

8 Bend the card into the hat shape and apply some glue to the card flap. Tuck this edge inside the hat so that the felt edges butt up together. Hold it until the glue has set. Trim any excess felt from the bottom edge.

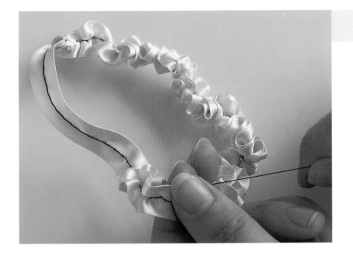

9 Stitch the two short edges of the narrow ribbon together to form a circle as a ruff for the bottom of the hat. Sew a row of gathering stitches down the centre of the ribbon right round the circle. Pull up the thread so that the ribbon forms neat ruffles, making the circle the same size as the bottom of the hat. Finish off the threads securely so that the gathering cannot come undone, then arrange the ruffles evenly for a neat appearance.

10 Using craft glue or a hot-glue gun, attach the gathered ribbon to the bottom of the hat. Adjust the ruffles so that they lie neatly, then leave to dry.

11 To finish off his costume, Harley has another ribbon ruff around his neck. This is made in the same way as the hat ruff, except that the gathering stitch is sewn along one edge of the ribbon. Slip the ribbon circle over Harley's head with the sewn edge closest to his neck. Gather up the ruff, adjusting it until it fits neatly around Harley's neck.

BABY ELLIE BEAR

This darling little bear is named after our great niece Ellie Rhiannon and would make a lovely gift for a new baby. Baby Ellie Bear's hands are specially shaped so she can be posed as if she is sucking her thumb, and her legs are designed to make her sit like a young child. She is wearing a cosy sleep-suit that is easily made from warm brushed cotton fabric.

you will need

- 50 x 75cm (20 x 30in), 12mm (½in) straight-pile mohair or synthetic fur fabric in natural white

- 20 x 25cm (8 x 10in), natural-white felt or Ultra-suede for the paws and pads

- Three, 35mm (1½in) plastic safety joints for the head and arms

- Two, 30mm (1¼in) plastic safety joints for the legs

- One pair, 12mm (½in) black plastic safety eyes

- 2m (2yds), black nose thread

- About 450g (1lb), polyester filling

- Sewing thread and strong thread to match

- Two, 150cm (6in) medium strength armatures for the arms (only to be used if the bear is NOT being given to a child to play with)

for the sleep-suit

- 80 x 112cm brushed cotton print fabric

- 50cm, 4mm wide white elastic (cut into 4 equal lengths)

- Three press-studs

- Sewing thread to match

22cm (8½in)

1 Use the templates on pages 91–96 to make patterns and cut out the pieces for Baby Ellie Bear as explained on pages 16–17. Make the head and body first following the guide on pages 17–18. Baby Ellie has a four-piece body. Turn both pieces right sides out and leave the body to one side ready for jointing later.

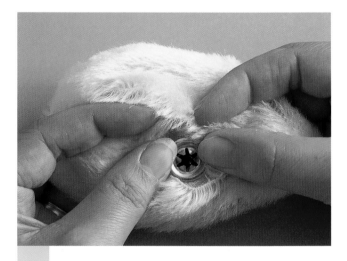

2 Attach the safety eyes to the head (see page 18). Make sure they are correctly positioned before attaching the star washer on each one. A good way to do this is to stuff the head loosely, position the eyes, remove the stuffing without disturbing them and secure the washers (see also page 17). Stuff the head firmly, attach the ears and embroider the nose (see pages 20–22).

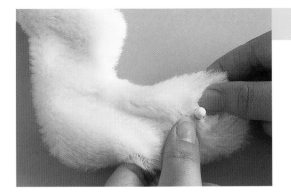

3 Baby Ellie's legs are designed to make her sit like a young child. Pin two of the leg pieces together and oversew the edges instead of tacking them. Leave the foot edge open as well as the opening marked on the pattern for turning. This opening is at the top of the leg on this design to ensure the joints can be inserted and the leg stuffed easily. Insert the footpad and stitch it in place neatly by hand since it will be visible on the finished bear. Now insert the joints (see page 20) and stuff the leg fairly firmly. Make the other leg in the same way and put both to one side ready for assembly later.

4 Baby Ellie has different shaped arms because she is designed to look as if she is sucking her thumb. Stitch the paw pad to the inner arm matching the straight edges, then carefully pin this inner arm to the corresponding outer arm with right sides together. Start pinning at the hand end making sure that the thumbs on the inner and outer arms match perfectly. Oversew the pinned pieces together to hold them in place before stitching them very carefully. Try to produce a smooth outline to form the shape of the thumb.

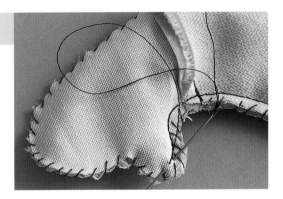

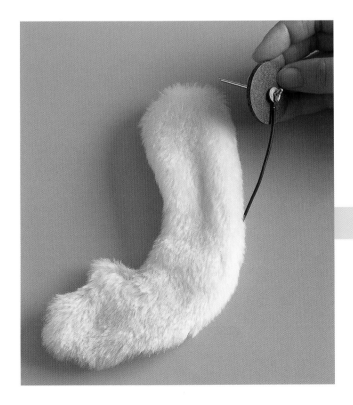

5 Joint and stuff the arms ready to be assembled as described on pages 20–21, closing the seams with ladder stitch. Use safety joints if you are making the bear for a child.

6 Alternatively, thread an armature onto the split pin supplied with traditional wooden joints and carefully slip it into the arm when the joint is being fitted. Then stuff the arm as before, making sure that the wire lies along the centre of the arm rather like a bone and cannot be felt at the tip of the hand.

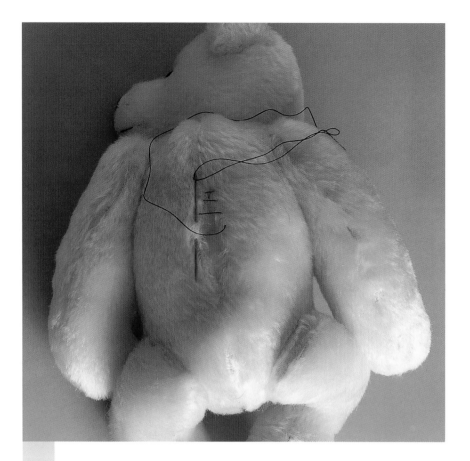

tip Always use plastic safety joints and plastic safety eyes when you are making a bear for a young child. If, however, a child won't be playing with your bear, you can incorporate an armature in the arm. This will allow you to bend Baby Ellie's arm so that her thumb is at her mouth and ensure it is kept in this position.

7 You are now ready to assemble Baby Ellie Bear (see page 23). First attach the head to the body at the point marked on the pattern, making sure you are happy that it looks right before securing it in place with the washer. Next fit the arms and then the legs in the same way. Check that the joints are securely fastened before stuffing the body, because it is much easier to adjust them now rather than when the bear is finished. Stuff the body firmly, filling the areas furthest from the opening first. Close the back seam with ladder stitch using extra strong thread (see page 21).

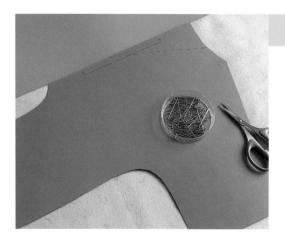

8 Cut out the pieces for the sleep-suit from your fabric using the templates on pages 91–92. Match the arrow on the pattern to the grain line or the direction of the fabric pattern where appropriate. Cut the back piece on the fold of the fabric to make one large piece or, if you prefer, cut your paper pattern on a fold to give you the finished pattern. Transfer the dart line on to the fabric.

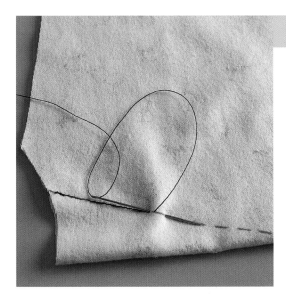

9 First stitch the dart. Fold the back piece in half with right sides together and pin at the neck edge and at the base of the dart. Stitch along the line of the dart, starting at the neck edge and finishing precisely at the point of the dart. Trim away the excess fabric and neaten the raw edges with zigzag stitch or by oversewing them to prevent fraying.

10 Place the two front pieces right sides together and stitch the short distance between points A and B. Press under the front edges to the wrong side and stitch in place close to the folded edge.

11 Open the front out flat and place over the back piece with right sides together. Stitch the sleep-suit together between points C to D, E to F, and under the legs from G to G. Neaten the neck edge by pressing the raw edge to the wrong side and stitching in place close to the folded edge.

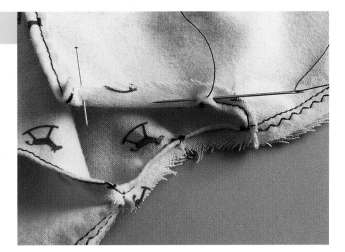

12 Press the fabric to the wrong side to make the casing for the elastic on the arms and legs, and stitch in place leaving a small gap to insert the elastic. Thread the elastic through the casing and securely join both ends together. Finish off the stitching of the casing when the elastic is in place. Finally sew on the press-studs to fasten Ellie's sleep-suit.

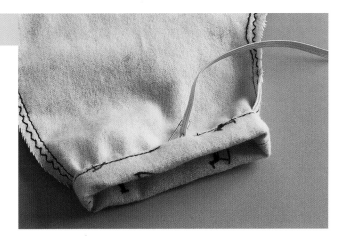

EMBROIDERED BEARS

These charming season bears are made from felt and finished off with a little embroidery. Felt is an excellent medium for making teddies because it is inexpensive and much easier to decorate in this way than other fabrics. Although this fabric is not suited to making a teddy for a child to play with, it will make an excellent display bear or christening present for when the child is older.

you will need

- *35 x 50cm (14 x 20in), high-quality felt in the colour of your choice – leaf green (spring), yellow (summer), tangerine (autumn) and pale blue (winter)*

- *35 x 50cm (14 x 20in), lightweight fusible interfacing*

- *20 x 20cm (8 x 8in), felt or Ultra-suede for the paws and pads*

- *Five, 25mm (1in) plastic safety joints*

- *One pair, 8mm black plastic safety eyes*

- *2m (2yds), black nose thread*

- *About 100g (3½oz), polyester filling*

- *Sewing thread and strong thread to match*

20cm (8in)

For the embroidery you will need the following Anchor stranded cottons

Spring
- *1 – white (daisy petals)*
- *46 – red (ladybird)*
- *90 – yellow (centres)*
- *403 – black (ladybird)*

Summer
- *260 – pale green (summer flowers)*
- *267 – green (summer flower leaves)*
- *290 – yellow (bee)*
- *342 – pale lilac (summer flowers)*
- *403 – black (bee)*
- *881 – pale dusky pink (summer flowers)*
- *895 – dusky pink (summer flowers)*

Autumn
- *362 – light brown (top of the acorn)*
- *375 – mid brown (base of the acorn)*

Winter
- *1 – white (snowflakes)*
- *46 – red (holly berries)*
- *246 – dark green (holly leaf)*

1 Use the templates on pages 97–99 to cut out the pieces for each embroidered bear as explained on page 16. Use a permanent marker pen to draw round the shapes on the felt. Felt does not have a grain direction so you do not have to worry about positioning the pieces precisely – simply fit them onto the fabric as close together as possible to reduce waste. Iron the interfacing to the back of each piece following the manufacturer's instructions to give the fabric extra strength and stability.

2 Make each bear following the guide on pages 16–23. Turn the body right sides out and stitch the embroidery before the bear is stuffed and jointed. Use all six strands of cotton unless otherwise specified. See pages 43–45 for a guide to the stitches used.

3 Insert the joints and stuffing before assembling each embroidered bear as explained in the bear-making guide on pages 20–23.

Autumn bear

You can embellish your felt bears with embroidery motifs or leave them completely plain, as you prefer. Templates for the motifs shown here are on page 99 and are easy to follow freehand. If you prefer to transfer them to the fabric beforehand, trace each motif with a transfer pencil and iron them onto the correct pieces before you sew the bear together. The stitches are straightforward to work and the sequence is described below. Practise on a spare piece of fabric before you add them to your bear.

Spring bear is decorated with bright daisies and ladybirds worked in a mixture of bullion stitch, straight stitch and French knots as described below.

Spring bear

Ladybird

Begin by making a bullion stitch about 7mm long using red thread.

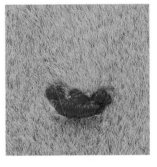

Work a row of five French knots just above this, first using red then with black stranded cotton.

Daisy

Using yellow thread, stitch French knots randomly across the body piece, keeping them well spaced.

Using white, form the daisy petals by working a series of straight stitches in a circle around each French knot.

Bring the needle out directly next to one of the yellow centres and take it down where you want the outer edge of the petal to go.

Bring it back up next to the yellow flower centre to add the next petal. Work 12 straight stitches in this way around each French knot.

Work another red bullion stitch above these French knots followed by another row of red and black French knots and then two further rows of red bullion stitch.

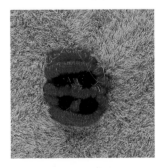

To make the ladybird's head, work a 5mm long bullion stitch using black thread. Finally, add six simple straight stitches for the ladybird's legs.

Summer bear's flowers and bees are created using the following stitches – stem, split and satin stitch as well as French knots. They are straightforward to work.

Summer bear

Flower

Bring the needle out where you want the base of your flower to go, and work the stems as shown in stem stitch using pale green thread.

When you have enough stems outline the shapes of the leaves in split stitch using green thread. Fill in these shapes with satin stitch. Work from one edge of the leaf to the centre as shown.

When this side of the leaf is complete, stitch from the other side to the centre to give the impression of a central vein on the leaf.

Add French knots to the top of each stem for the flowers. Use a random mix of dusky pink, pale dusky pink and pale lilac.

Bee

The bee is worked in a similar way to the ladybird on the Spring bear.

Start with a bullion stitch measuring about 6mm across at the base of the bee using black thread. Work another bullion stitch above this stitch using yellow thread. Follow on with three more rows of bullion stitch, using first black, then yellow then black again.

Stitch two French knots close together near the centre of the top of the body to show the head using black thread. To finish off, add wings to the bee by working lazy daisy stitches in one strand of black thread. Make the top wings slightly larger than the bottom wings.

Autumn bear is decorated with a few simple acorns. These are created using a mixture of French knots, split stitch and satin stitch.

Acorns

Work a row of three French knots in mid brown thread close together for the base of the shell. Above this add another two rows of five French knots. Fill any gaps with extra French knots.

Using light brown thread, draw the outline of the acorn above the shell in split stitch then fill it in with satin stitch.

Winter bear

Winter bear's snowflakes are probably the easiest motifs of all to work. Stitch them randomly across his body and add a holly leaf to his foot pad.

Snowflakes

Make some of the snowflakes smaller than others and space them randomly to prevent the design from looking too symmetrical. You can also make up your own more complex snowflake design.

The snowflakes on the Winter bear's body are created by working a series of straight stitches in white thread. Make the three long straight stitches that form the main structure of the snowflake cross in the middle.

Add small straight stitches in a diagonal direction at each end of the long straight stitches.

Holly leaf

The holly leaf on the Winter bear's foot is worked in the same way as the leaves on the summer flowers. First outline the shape of the leaf with split stitch then fill it in with satin stitch using dark green thread.

On this small scale it is not easy to outline the pointed, sharp edges of the leaf, so these are easily added by extending one stitch beyond the outline at regular intervals. Work from the edges to the centre again to give the impression of a central vein. Stitch five French knots at the base of the holly leaf for the holly berries using red thread.

BRACKEN BEAR

This unusual teddy has hand-painted eyes and a multi-coloured nose in shades to match her beautiful lilac fur. She also knows how to keep a secret because she has a hidden compartment sewn into her tummy where you can put a small diary or some letters. What a wonderful gift to make for a friend.

you will need

- *70 x 50cm (27 x 20in), 12mm (½ in) straight-pile mohair or synthetic fur fabric in lilac*

- *30 x 30cm (12 x 12in), felt or ultra-suede for the paws, pads, inner ears and back compartment in natural white*

- *Three, 50mm (2in) plastic safety joints for the head and arms*

- *Two, 35mm (1½ in) plastic safety joints for the legs*

- *One pair, 16mm (⅝ in) clear plastic safety eyes with black pupils*

- *Purple acrylic or enamel paint for the eyes*

- *About 2m (2¼ yds), black nose thread*

- *Two shades of lilac embroidery thread for the nose – about 1m of each*

- *Small piece of black felt or ultra-suede for the nose template*

- *About 450g (1lb), polyester filling*

- *Sewing thread and strong thread to match*

38cm (15 n)

tip If you paint the eyes yourself you can match the colour to the shade of your fur and nose thread, making your bear totally exclusive. You can of course buy eyes in your chosen shade instead if you prefer.

1 Use the patterns on pages 100–105 to make templates and cut out the pieces for Bracken Bear as explained in the step-by-step guide on pages 16–17. Before you stitch the bear together, paint the backs of the clear eyes with lilac non-toxic acrylic or enamel paint to give them their unique colour. Clean the backs of the eyes with white spirit to remove any fingerprints, then using a fine brush, carefully paint the back of each eye ensuring that the paint does not creep over the edges to the front. Allow to dry thoroughly.

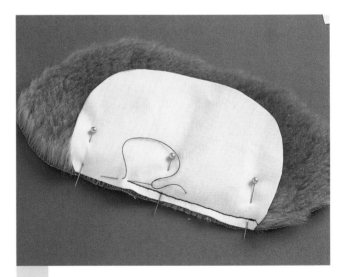

2 Make the head, arms and legs as described on pages 17–19. The body is assembled as follows. With right sides together, place one of the ultra-suede or felt compartment pieces on top of one of the back pieces, lining up the straight edge with the reference marks on the back piece. Stitch in place using a slightly narrower seam than usual. Repeat this with the remaining back and compartment pieces.

3 Open out the stitched back pieces. Pin one on top of the other with right sides together, matching the raw edges of the fur body and the edges of the compartment. Oversew along this edge from the top, around the curved compartment edge and down to the bottom to hold it securely in place, leaving the side seams open. Stitch the pieces together.

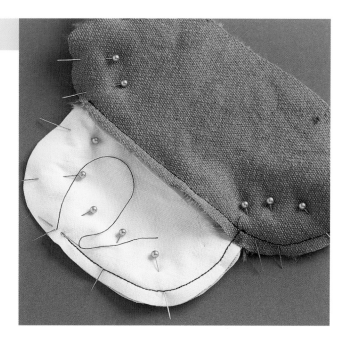

4 Join the two front body pieces along the front edge, leaving the opening marked on the pattern for turning and stuffing. Place the front and back pieces right sides together, matching the seams at the top and bottom of the body. Pin in position and oversew the edges. As an opening has been left in the front seam, you can stitch the body together all round the edge. The secret compartment should be protruding from the back so make sure that you do not catch it in your stitching. Turn the body right side out and tuck the compartment inside.

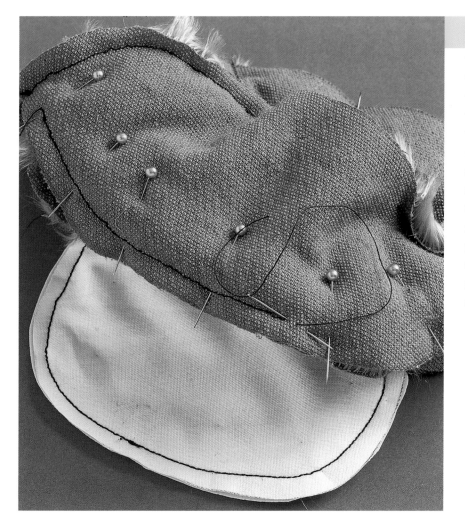

5 The bear can now be jointed as described on page 20. You may find it fiddly because of the secret compartment inside the body. When all the joints are in place, the body cavity is ready to be filled. Add the polyester filling gradually, keeping one hand inside the secret compartment to help you judge how much filling is needed. Avoid stuffing too firmly so you can fit treasures inside the bear.

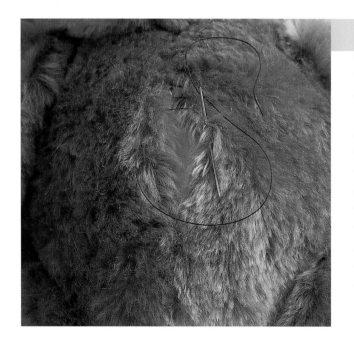

6 When you are happy with the way the bear looks, close the front seam neatly with ladder stitch. Thread a needle with extra strong thread and knot the end. Anchor the knot inside the body at the top of the opening. Make a small stitch along the same side of the opening, then take the needle across to the opposite side and pull the thread tight until the edges are drawn together. Continue taking small stitches and then crossing over to the other side in this way until the gap is closed. Finish off securely.

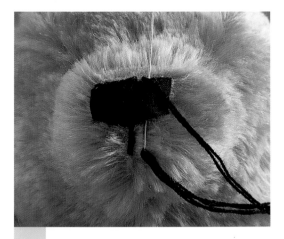

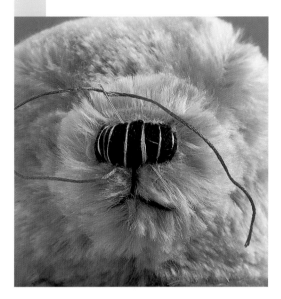

8 Using the lighter of the two contrasting embroidery threads, make three equally spaced stitches over the nose, on each side of the long central stitch. With the darker thread add more stitches to the nose between the light stitches until you are happy with the effect.

7 Bracken has a multi-coloured nose. You can also use this technique on any of the other bears if you wish. First, embroider the nose following the instructions on pages 21–22 using black nose thread.

Bracken Bear is made with a secret compartment in her back which you can use to store your treasures. The compartment is made from felt or ultra-suede, although you could also use a fabric of your own choice. If you wish to leave out the secret compartment altogether, make the four-piece body as explained on page 19.

TEDDY EDWARD BEAR

This cuddly little chap is in the
style of the traditional bears
made in the 1950s and 1960s.
He is made from old gold fur,
which was a very popular
colour at the time. If you
cannot find this shade he will
look just as charming in an
alternative colour. This little
bear is very straightforward to
make and an ideal first project
if you are new to making toys.

you will need

■ *70 x 50cm (27 x 20in), 12mm (½in) straight-pile mohair or synthetic fur fabric in old gold*

■ *20 x 15cm (8 x 6in), felt or ultra-suede for the paws and pads, in beige*

■ *Five, 36mm (1½in) plastic safety joints*

■ *One pair, 13mm (½in) amber plastic safety eyes with black pupils*

■ *About 2m (2¼yds), black nose thread*

■ *Small piece of black felt for the nose template*

■ *About 450g (1lb), polyester filling*

■ *One, medium-size growler, about 50mm (2in) diameter*

■ *Sewing thread and strong thread to match*

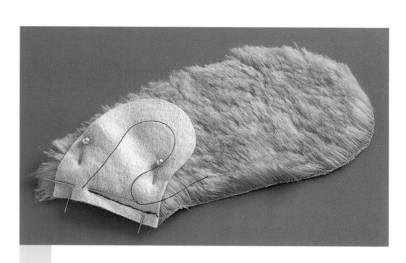

1 Use the templates on page 106–110 to cut out the pieces for Teddy Edward Bear following the instructions in the step-by-step guide on page 16–17. Place one felt or ultra-suede pad on top of each inner arm with right sides together and the straight edges level. Pin in place, then oversew the edges to prevent them from moving during stitching. Sew the paw pad securely in position.

33cm (13in)

2 Join the inner and outer arms together. Pin the two pieces right sides together ensuring that the outer edges are level and there are no puckers in the fabric and tucking in the pile as you go (see page 26). Stitch all around the arm, starting at one of the points marked on the pattern and finishing at the other point, leaving a gap in between for turning and stuffing. If using a sewing machine, stitch the seams twice for added strength.

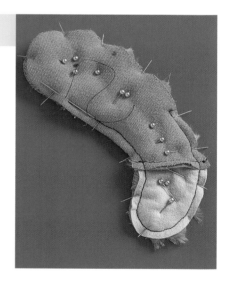

3 Turn the arm right side out and make a hole using an awl for the joint (see page 15) at the point marked on the pattern. Put one half of the safety joint inside the arm and push the shank through the hole to the outside. Stuff the arm firmly and close with ladder stitch (see page 21). The legs are assembled in the same way except that the footpad needs to be inserted. This is explained on page 19.

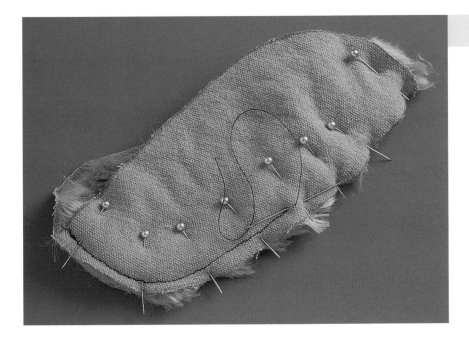

4 Make the head as explained on pages 17–18. Attach the safety eyes before stuffing. Check the body pieces are the right way up before stitching each front piece to a back piece along the side seams. Pin these sections together at the top and bottom of the body, matching the seams as reference points. Pin and oversew the remaining edges together and stitch in place, leaving the opening marked on the pattern.

5 When the pieces have been sewn, they can be jointed and stuffed, ready for assembly (see pages 20–21). The head should be joined to the body first because it is the reference point for everything else. Make a hole in the body at the point marked on the pattern for the head joint. Pass the shank of the joint through the hole and, from the inside of the body, secure it in place with the other half of the joint and the washer. Attach each limb in the same way checking that the arms and the legs are level and the same distance away from the head.

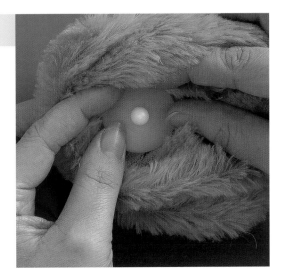

6 All that remains is to stuff the body, however on a traditional teddy it is a nice idea to add a growler as well. First, place a generous amount of stuffing in the tummy so that the growler will not be felt from the outside. Place the growler flat in the cavity with the holes facing backwards towards the open seam (this will make the bear growl when he is tipped forward). Continue adding more stuffing around and over the growler until the body is firmly stuffed. Close the seam with ladder stitch (see page 21).

MUZZWELL BEAR

The body, muzzle and ears of this handsome two-tone bear are in a much lighter shade than his limbs and head. This teddy may look complicated to make, but is quite straightforward, even for a novice bear-maker. His nose is made from a fabric-covered piece of plastic threaded with a safety eye, which saves having to embroider one.

you will need

- *70 x 50cm (27 x 20in), 18mm (¾in) straight-pile mohair or synthetic fur fabric in copper*

- *35 x 50cm (14 x 20in), 12mm (½in) straight-pile mohair or synthetic fur fabric in gold*

- *30 x 30cm (12 x 12in), felt or ultra-suede for the paws and pads, in fawn*

- *8 x 8cm (3 x 3in), felt or ultra-suede for covering the nose, in dark brown*

- *4 x 4cm (1½ x 1½in), stout plastic for the nose*

- *One, 18mm (¾in) plastic safety eye with washer for the nose*

- *Five, 50mm (2in) plastic safety joints*

- *One pair, 16mm (⅝in) amber plastic safety eyes with black pupils*

- *About 2m (2¼yds), black nose thread*

- *About 700g (1½lb), polyester filling*

- *Sewing thread and strong thread to match*

38cm (15in)

tip This bear would look good made in other coloured fabrics, too – for example, in a child's favourite colours. Remember to pick two shades that will give a good contrast between light and dark – this is important to the design. You can also reverse the shades or introduce a third colour if you wish.

1 Use the templates on page 111–115 to cut out the pieces for Muzzwell Bear from your chosen fabrics as explained on pages 16–17. Refer to the individual pattern pieces for which colour fabric to use.

2 Place the gold head gusset piece on top of the copper head gusset piece with the fur sides together and the straight edges level. Pin along this edge and oversew in position before stitching securely in place.

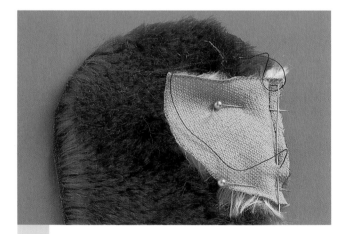

3 Now join the head side pieces. Place a contrast gold head piece on top of a copper main head piece with fur sides together matching the grain direction and the straight edge A. Pin and oversew the pieces, then sew together securely. Repeat with the other head side pieces.

4 The two head pieces can now be partially joined by placing one head on top of the other head with fur sides together, ensuring the seams between the two colours are matching. Pin and oversew these pieces together along the curved underchin seam and stitch in place.

5 Now carefully insert the head gusset. Match the seams between the different colours so that the muzzle has a smooth outline and the finished effect will not be spoilt by the colours being staggered. First, line up the seam on one side of the head with the seam on the head gusset and pin in position. Do the same on the other side of the head and pin in place.

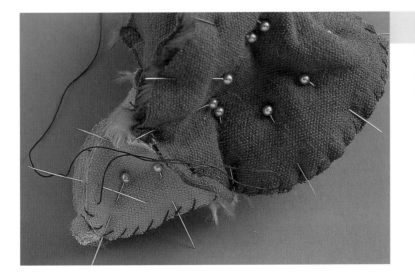

6 Oversew the pieces together at these points to prevent the fabric from moving. Continue pinning the head gusset in place, oversew the edges and stitch securely in place.

MUZZWELL BEAR **59**

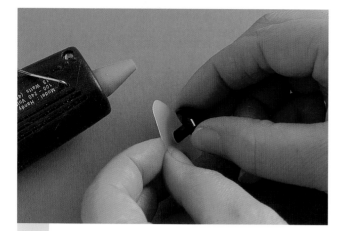

7 Cut out the small nose shape from an ice-cream tub or any stout plastic container with a flat surface. Make sure the edges of the plastic are smooth once you have cut out the nose, sanding them if necessary. Make a hole right in the centre of the nose large enough to take the stalk of the safety eye using a hole punch. Insert the plastic eye and secure it with a blob of glue.

8 This lump of plastic now needs to be covered. Cut the nose cover from felt or ultra suede and using strong thread, run a gathering stitch (a large running stitch) around the edge. Pull up the threads so that the fabric is cupped ready to cover the plastic nose. To prevent any hard edges showing through, put a small amount of polyester stuffing inside the fabric. Place the plastic nose inside the cover ensuring that the stuffing adequately pads it from the front and sides.

9 Keeping a firm hold on the stalk of the eye, pull up the threads firmly until the fabric is gathered around the base and any puckers that may have appeared on the front of the nose have gone. Take a look at the nose from the front to make sure it is correctly stuffed and the fabric is nice and smooth. You can easily rearrange it at this stage if you are not happy with it. When you have finished, stitch the fabric in position.

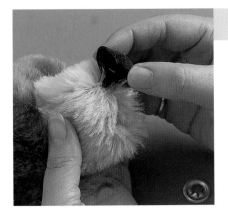

10 Turn the head right side out. Find the junction where the head gusset seam meets the under-chin seam of the head and make a hole with an awl just above the stitches (this avoids breaking the seam, which would cause problems later). Pass the stalk of your new nose through the hole and, from the inside of the head, attach the washer to hold it in place. This washer must be attached very securely to ensure that the nose cannot be pulled off. One way to do this is by placing an empty cotton reel over the washer and giving it a good bash with a hammer.

11 Attach the safety eyes, stuff the head and attach the ears; make the limbs and body and assemble your bear as described in the step-by-step guide on pages 18–23.

12 When he is finished Muzzwell will really benefit from a final grooming with a teasel brush, as this will release any of the pile that has been trapped in the seams. Take extra care around the eyes, as the wire bristles will scratch the surface, spoiling their glossy finish.

JOLLY BEAR

This gorgeous teddy is an ideal bedtime companion because he is so cuddly. He is made from very soft, mahogany-coloured fur and has a great big, saggy tummy. Jolly's legs are stitched straight onto the body but the arms and head are jointed in the usual way.

you will need

■ *50 x 137cm (19 x 54in), 12mm (½in) distressed-pile mohair in mahogany*

■ *15 x 20cm (6 x 8in), felt or ultra-suede for the paws and pads*

■ *Two, 36mm (1½in) plastic safety joints for the arms*

■ *One, 50mm (2in) plastic safety joint for the head*

■ *One pair, 10mm (⅜in) amber plastic safety eyes with black pupils*

■ *About 2m (2¼yds), black nose thread*

■ *Small piece of black felt for the nose template*

■ *About 450g (1lb), polyester filling*

■ *Sewing thread and strong thread to match*

35cm (14in)

tip **Jolly's huge tummy is ideal for adding a growler (or musical movement if he is not intended as a toy for a young child). Remember to leave enough space for it when stuffing the body.**

1 Use the templates on pages 116–119 to cut out the pieces for Jolly Bear as explained on pages 16–17. First, attach the legs to the body pieces. Matching points A and B marked on the patterns, pin one leg piece to each of the body pieces. Oversew in position to prevent the fabric from moving and stitch in place.

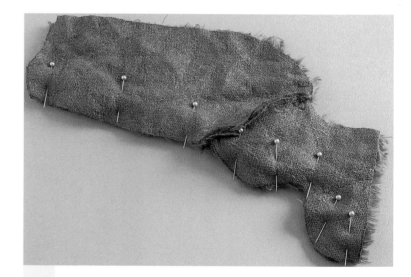

2 Next, join the body pieces together. Place one body front piece over its corresponding body back with fur sides together. Pin along the side seam and around the leg, matching the edges carefully. Oversew in position then carefully stitch along this side seam from the top neck edge to the toe of the foot, then along the inside of the leg to the base of the body. This will leave the bottom of the foot open ready to fit the foot pad later.

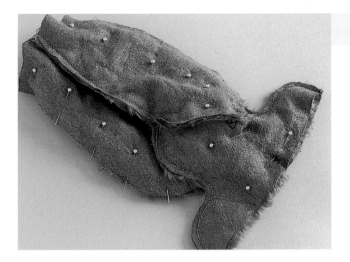

3 Repeat step 2 with the other body front and back pieces. Then join the two body halves. Pin first the body fronts together then the body backs, with fur sides together and matching the raw edges carefully. Oversew in position then stitch in place around the body leaving the neck edge open. Remember to leave the gap in the back marked on the pattern for turning. Make sure that enough fabric is caught in the seam when stitching between the legs. Stitch the foot pads in place as described in the step-by-step guide on page 19 before turning the body the right way out.

4 Make Jolly's head as described on page 17. Turn the completed head right side out and attach the plastic safety eyes. Stuff the head firmly, insert a safety joint, and gather the neck edge with extra strong thread to secure it. Make the ears and attach them to the head with ladder stitch as described on page 21. You can either embroider the nose with nose thread or add a plastic safety nose, but remember to attach this with the eyes before stuffing.

5 Using extra-strong thread, run a large gathering stitch (this is just a running stitch) along the neck edge of the body. Pull these stitches up tightly, tucking the raw edges to the inside of the body, and leaving a hole large enough for the shank of the head joint to pass through. Finish off the ends very securely. Fix the head in place as described on page 23.

6 Make the arms as described in the step-by-step guide on page 19. Attach the completed arms to the body at the points marked on the pattern making sure that the arms are facing to the front (it is easy to put them on the wrong way around).

7 All that remains now is to stuff the body and legs. Start by adding filler to the feet first as this is the hardest part to reach. Continue adding filling until the body is as soft or as firm as you would like. Finally, close the back seam with ladder stitch and give Jolly a good brush to lift the fur pile from the seams.

SLEEPING BEAR

This little bear has wonderful sleepy eyes and no moving parts at all. He is quick and easy to make without the need for any joints, and is the perfect choice for a last-minute gift. The sleepy eyelids are easy to make and attach to plastic safety eyes, but can be left out if you prefer.

you will need

- *35 x 100cm (14 x 39in), 16mm (⅝in) tipped straight-pile German mohair in fawn with brown tip*

- *15 x 25cm (6 x 10in), ultra-suede for the underbody and eyelids*

- *One pair, 13mm (½ in) black plastic safety eyes*

- *About 225g (½lb), polyester filling*

- *About 2m (2¼yds), black nose thread*

- *Sewing thread and strong thread to match*

33cm (13in)

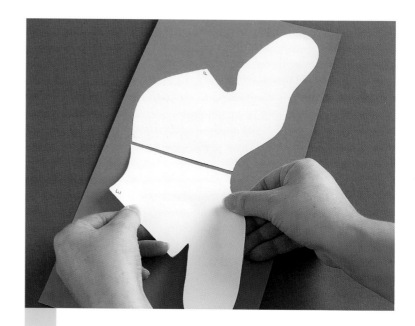

1 You will find the templates for Sleeping Bear on pages 120–122. Before you can start transferring them to the fabric, you need to join together the two halves of the main body pattern piece along the dotted lines, matching the edges as precisely as you can. Then make up your cardboard templates and cut out the pieces from the fabric as explained on pages 16–17, taking care to follow the arrows indicating the pile direction.

2 First attach the legs to the underbody. Pin the front legs to the underbody with right sides facing and matching the letters A and B on the patterns. Oversew to hold the pieces in place then stitch securely in position. Attach the back legs in the same way to the underbody, this time matching the letters C and D.

3 With fur sides facing, pin the two main body pieces together along the top edge between points E and F. The fur pile is quite long on this design, and should be tucked to the inside as you work to prevent the seams from showing on the finished bear. Oversew to hold in place then stitch securely in position between these points only.

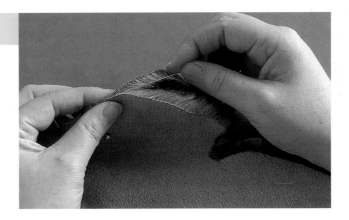

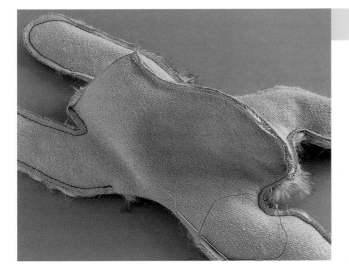

4 Attach the body piece to the underbody. Start by matching the front legs on the upper and under bodies and pinning them together. Next pin the back legs together then continue around the entire body leaving both the neck edge open and also the opening marked on the pattern for turning. Oversew to hold the pieces together then stitch in place. Do not turn right side out yet.

5 The head has a small dart at each side on the bottom edge. These are used instead of a joint and give the bottom of the head a more rounded form. Bring the edges of the dart together on each head piece with fur sides facing, and stitch in place. Repeat with the other head piece, then continue to make the head as described on page 17.

6 Make the eyelids and attach them to the eyes before fixing the eyes in position. Cut out the eyelid pieces from the template on page 122. Make a hole with an awl in the eyelid back in the position marked on the pattern, then place one eyelid front on top of an eye back with right sides together. Carefully hand stitch around the upper curved edge in a 3mm seam. Turn the right side out.

7 Attach the eyelid to the eye by passing the shank of the safety eye through the hole in the eyelid back and tucking the eye under the upper lid. Repeat with the other eyelid. Turn the head right side out and fix the eyes in position as described on pages 17–18. If you wish to use a plastic safety nose remember to attach it now.

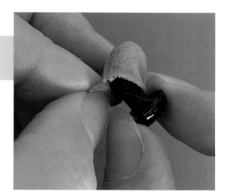

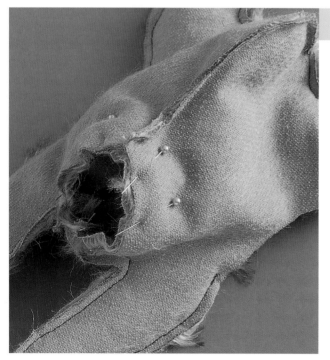

8 It's easy to attach the head to the body on this bear, however the head must be facing front. To make our little bear look like he's resting on his paws we turned his head slightly to one side. With the body inside out and the head right side out, push the top of the head down into the body until the neck edges of both the head and body are lined up. Turn the head until one of the darts matches the front edge of the underbody. This will position the head so that it is slightly turned and ensure that it is facing forwards. Oversew the edges together then stitch the head securely in place.

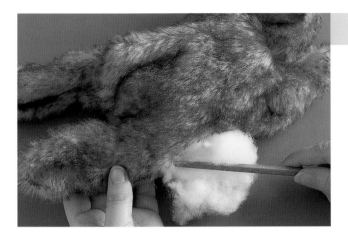

9 Turn the bear right side out through the opening in the side – this is a little fiddly but it is possible. Starting with the legs, stuff the bear softly to keep his cuddly appearance and gradually fill the body to finish. Close the seam with ladder stitch (see page 21).

10 Make and attach the ears, and embroider the nose if you have not already added a plastic safety one (see page 21–22).

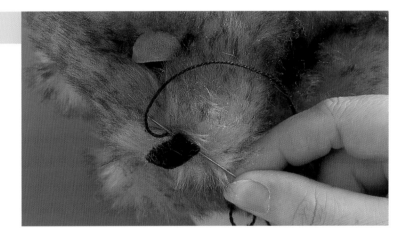

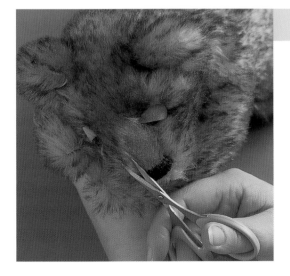

11 Sleeping Bear's lovely pale coloured muzzle is achieved by removing the tipped ends of the fur pile to reveal the pale fur underneath. Trim the ends of the pile very slowly and carefully around the muzzle area. Cut off small amounts at a time until you are happy with the way your bear looks.

12 If you would prefer your bear's head to move, you can easily insert a joint by following step 5 on page 65.

Baby's First Bear

A teddy is the most popular first toy given to a child. This delightful little chap will make an extra special gift for a new child or grandchild, and is sure to be treasured. He is made from a very short pile mohair fabric that is easy to clean and ideal for a baby's toy. The pattern can be reduced to make a miniature bear older children and adults will love.

you will need

- *15 x 100cm (6 x 39in), 6mm (¼in) straight-pile mohair in pale pink or pale blue*

- *10 x 10cm (4 x 4in), ultra-suede or felt in natural white*

- *Five, 20mm (¾in) plastic safety joints*

- *One pair, 7.5mm plastic safety eyes*

- *About 100 grams (4oz) polyester filling*

- *Sewing thread and strong thread to match*

- *About 1m (39in), black nose thread*

18cm (7in)

tip **The head on this bear is slightly different because the ears are sewn into small slits cut in the side of the head pieces. This means that the ears will always be symmetrical but does not allow you to position them to give a different look to your teddy's face. If you prefer to attach the ears in the normal way, do not cut the slits in the side of the head.**

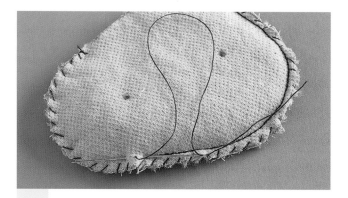

1 Use the templates on pages 123–124 to cut out the pieces for Baby's First Bear as explained in the step-by-step guide on pages 16–17. As he is the smallest design in this collection, you may find it easier to use embroidery scissors to cut out the intricate shapes. You may also prefer to stitch the entire bear by hand rather than to manoeuvre the sewing machine around the small pieces. Use a smaller seam allowance of 4–5mm.

2 This charming little bear is made as described in the step-by-step guide on pages 16–23 except for the head. Make up the body, arms and legs and turn them right sides out. Place the joints into the arms and legs, stuff them quite softly and close the final seams with ladder stitch using extra-strong thread (see page 21).

3 Make each ear by putting two ear pieces right sides together and stitching round the curved edge. Turn right sides out and close the bottom straight edge with ladder stitch or slipstitch. Place an ear on top of each head piece with fur sides together and matching the straight edge of the ear to one of the cut edges of the slit (with the curved edge of the ear pointing towards the back of the head). As the slit is only about two-thirds as long as the ear, the rest of the ear should extend beyond the top of the head.

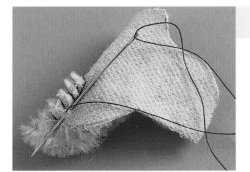

4 Now, with right sides together, fold the head piece in half, bringing the nose over to meet the back edge, and sandwiching the ear in the middle. Oversew the ear in position and securely stitch in place.

5 The top of the ear will still be sticking up out of the top of the head. Bend this part of the ear forwards towards the nose, matching the straight edge of the ear to the raw edge of the head and oversew it in place to hold it securely. This part of the ear is stitched in place when the head gusset is inserted as explained in step 4 on page 17.

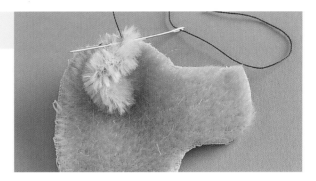

6 Fix in place the plastic safety eyes (see page 17) and stuff the head firmly to aid the embroidery of the nose. If you would rather use a safety nose, fix this in place before stuffing. If you want to give your bear a softer finish stuff the head a little less firmly. Secure the joint inside the head ready for assembly and embroider the nose if you have not used a plastic one (see pages 20–22).

7 Attach the head to the body as shown in the step-by-step guide on page 23, followed by the arms and then the legs. When all the limbs are securely fastened in place, the tummy cavity can be filled.

8 You can give the little bear a voice by including a small squeaker in his tummy. Insert enough stuffing at the front of the tummy to ensure the squeaker cannot be felt from the outside. Place the squeaker in the tummy with a flat side facing forwards. Continue adding filler until the body is softly filled yet squashy enough for the squeaker to be operated. Close the final seam with ladder stitch.

To make a tiny bear measuring just 13cm (5in), reduce the templates on pages 123–4 by 50%. You can also personalise your bear by adding a heart-shaped patch as shown here.

TEMPLATES

In this section you will find the patterns you need to make the bears described in this book. These can be traced and made into cardboard templates as explained in the step-by-step guide on page 16.

You will notice that some of the patterns need to be enlarged on a photocopier before you can use them. The percentage to use is listed on the relevant pattern pieces.

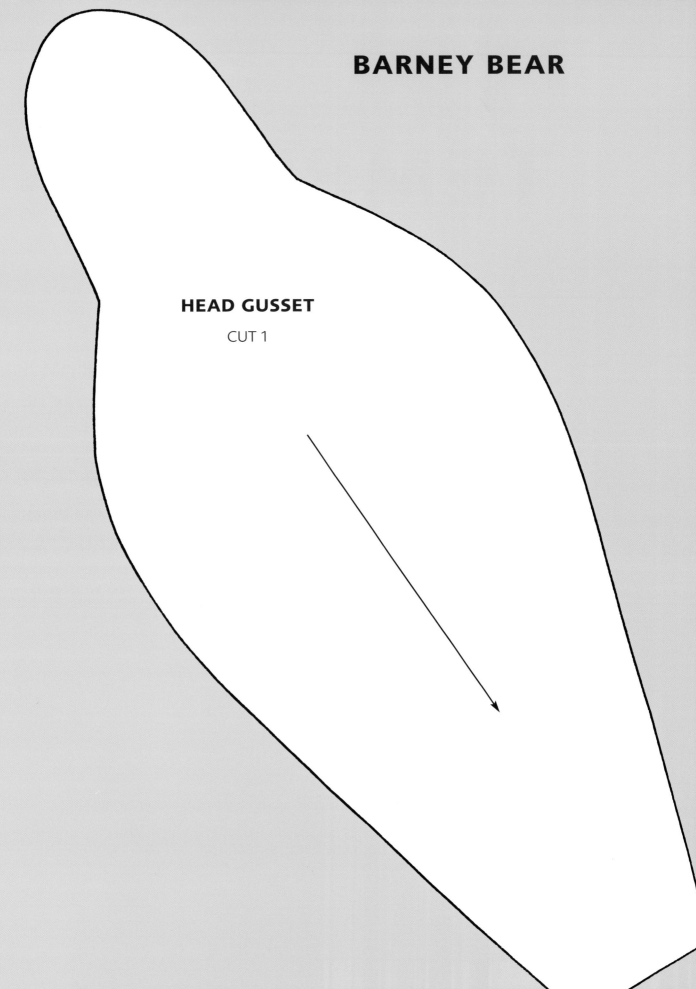

BARNEY BEAR

HEAD GUSSET

CUT 1

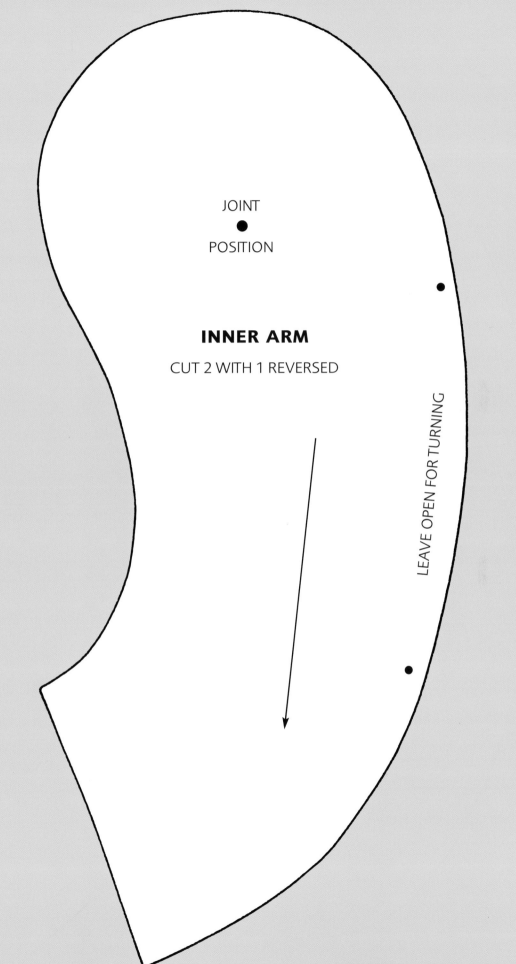

JOINT

POSITION

INNER ARM

CUT 2 WITH 1 REVERSED

LEAVE OPEN FOR TURNING

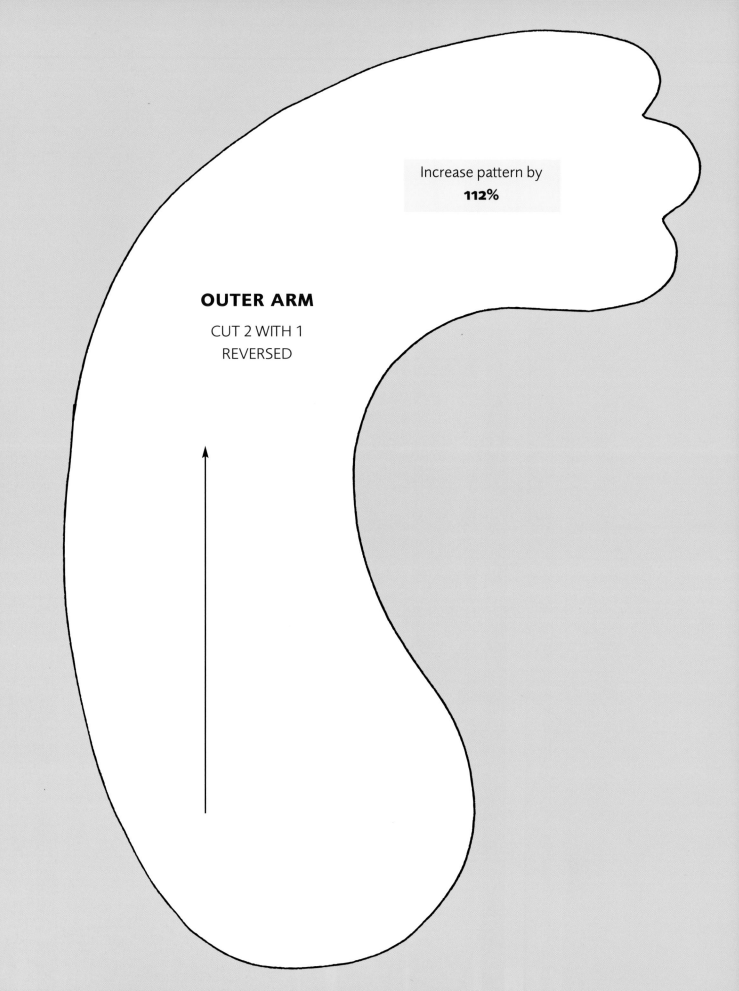

Increase pattern by
112%

OUTER ARM

CUT 2 WITH 1
REVERSED

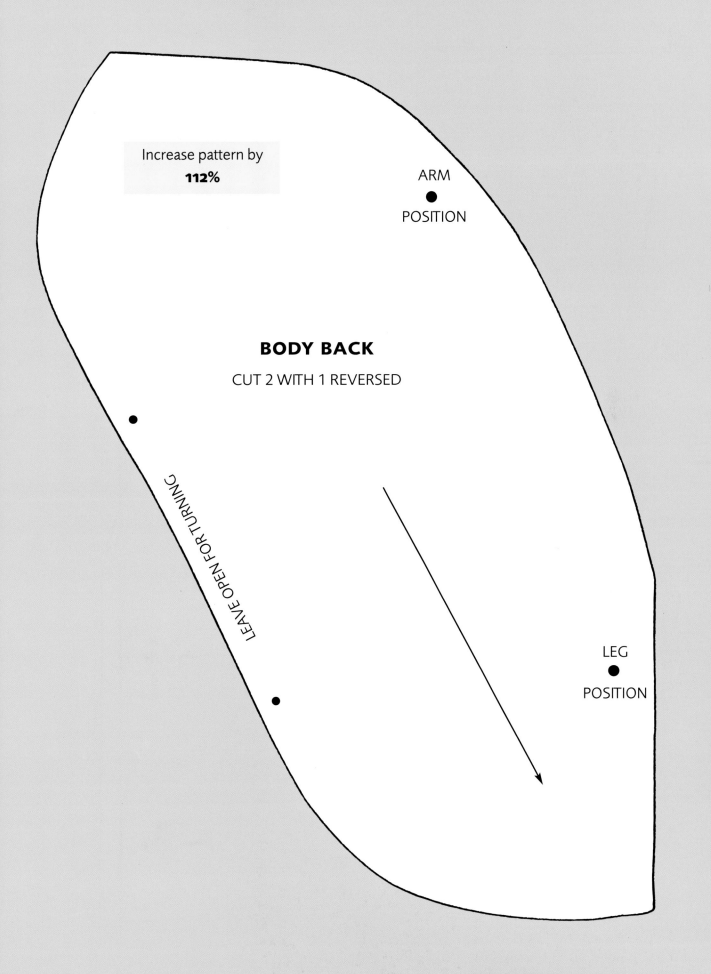

Increase pattern by
112%

ARM
●
POSITION

BODY BACK

CUT 2 WITH 1 REVERSED

LEAVE OPEN FOR TURNING

LEG
●
POSITION

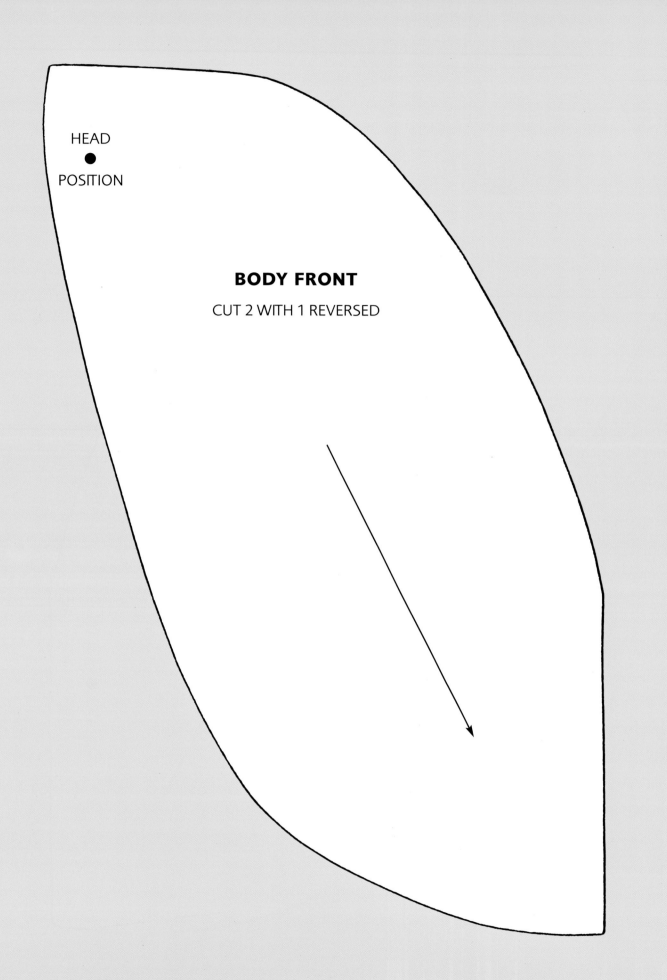

HEAD

POSITION

BODY FRONT

CUT 2 WITH 1 REVERSED

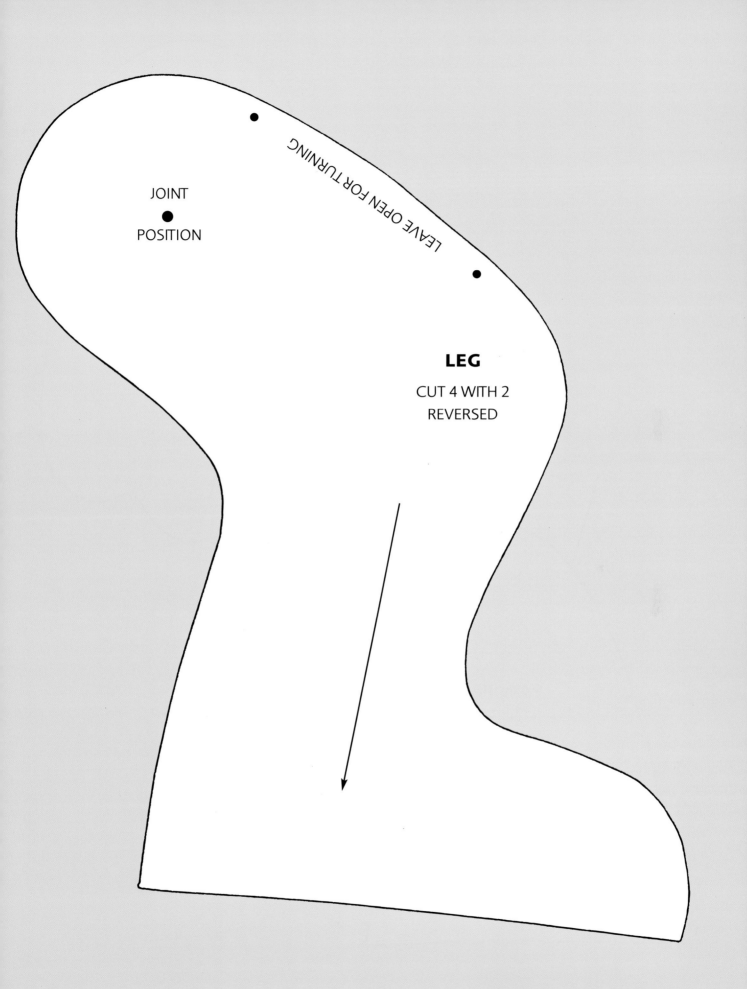

JOINT

POSITION

LEAVE OPEN FOR TURNING

LEG

CUT 4 WITH 2
REVERSED

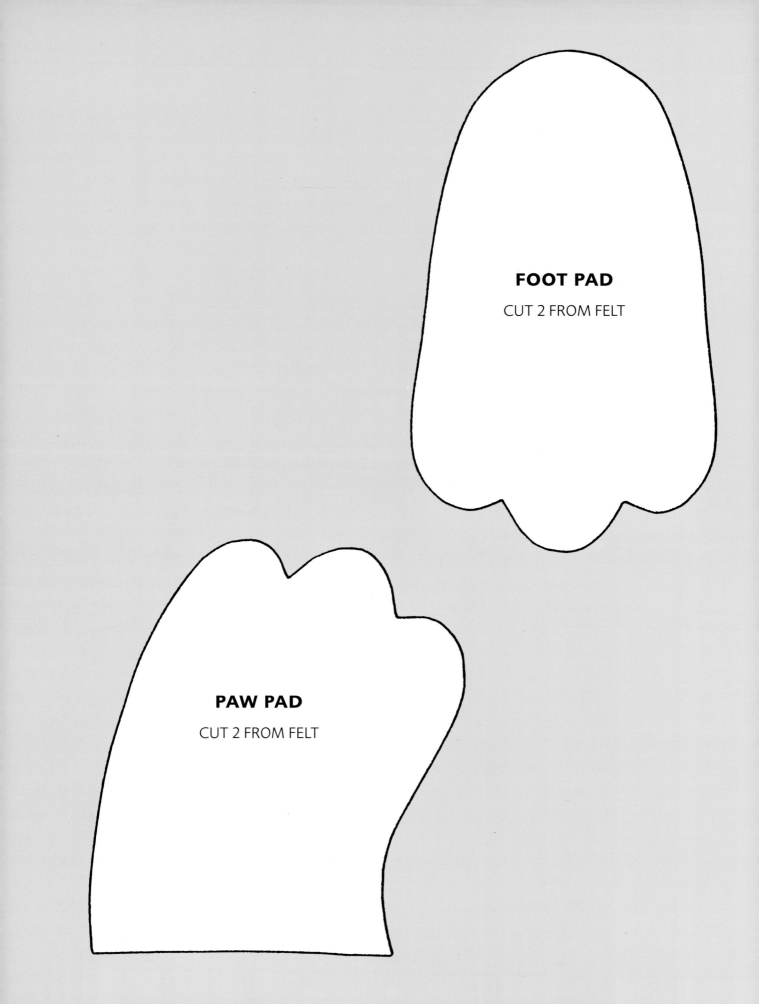

FOOT PAD

CUT 2 FROM FELT

PAW PAD

CUT 2 FROM FELT

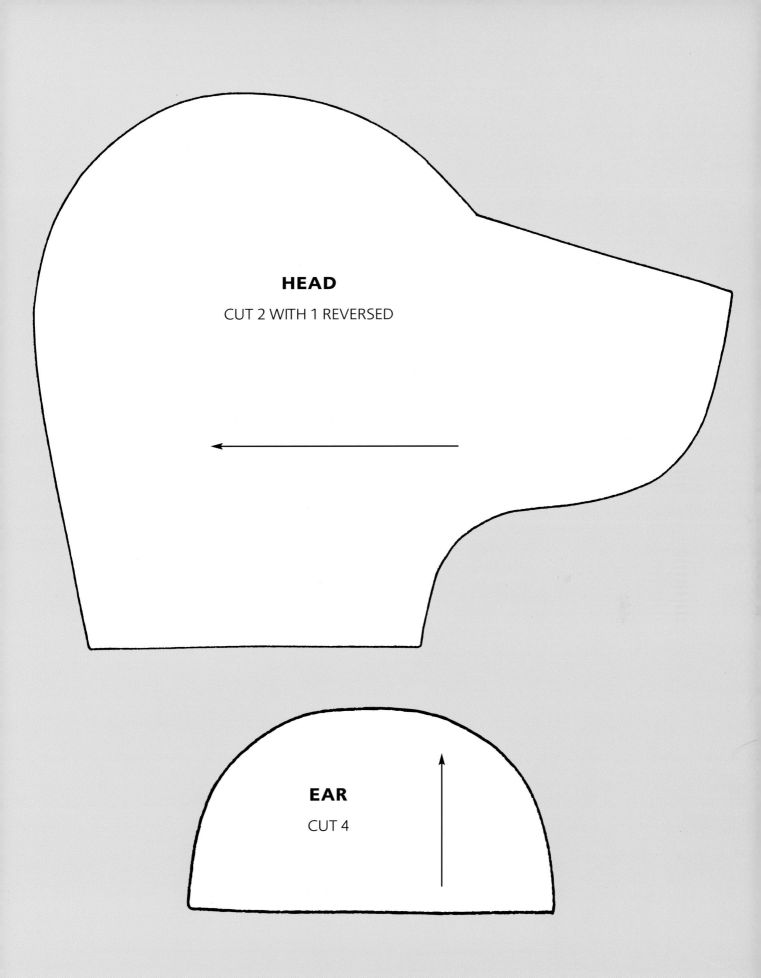

HEAD

CUT 2 WITH 1 REVERSED

EAR

CUT 4

HARLEY THE CLOWN BEAR

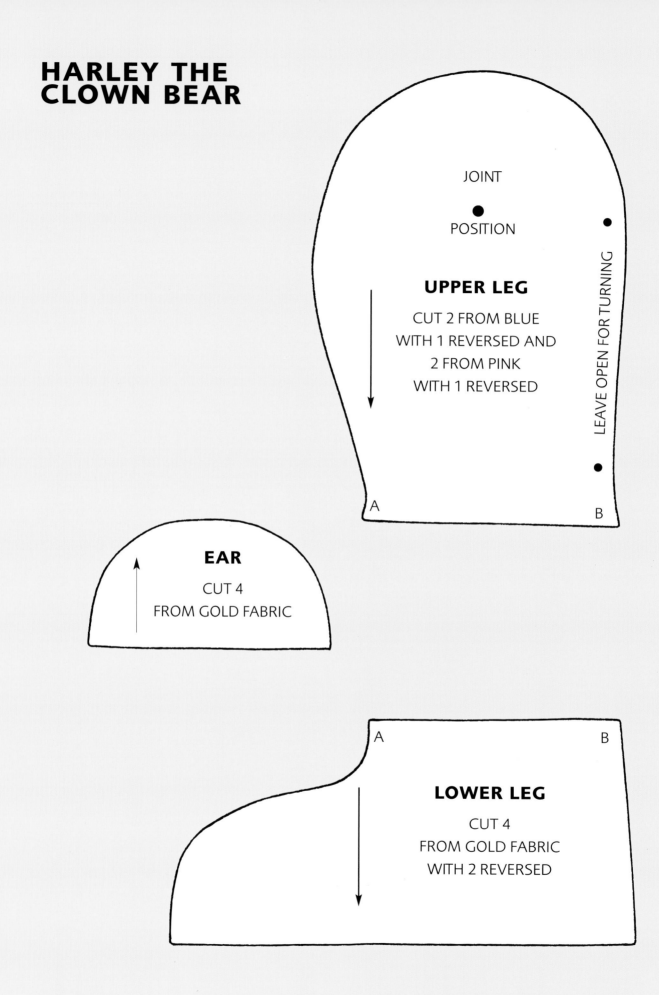

JOINT

●

POSITION

UPPER LEG

CUT 2 FROM BLUE
WITH 1 REVERSED AND
2 FROM PINK
WITH 1 REVERSED

LEAVE OPEN FOR TURNING

A   B

EAR

CUT 4
FROM GOLD FABRIC

A   B

LOWER LEG

CUT 4
FROM GOLD FABRIC
WITH 2 REVERSED

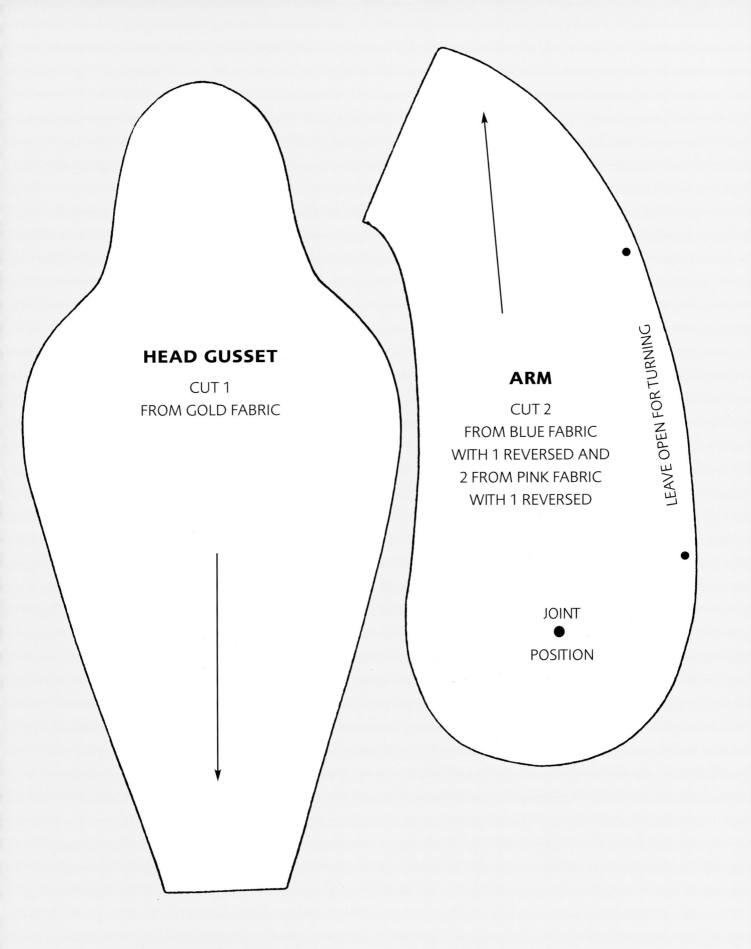

HEAD GUSSET

CUT 1
FROM GOLD FABRIC

ARM

CUT 2
FROM BLUE FABRIC
WITH 1 REVERSED AND
2 FROM PINK FABRIC
WITH 1 REVERSED

LEAVE OPEN FOR TURNING

JOINT

POSITION

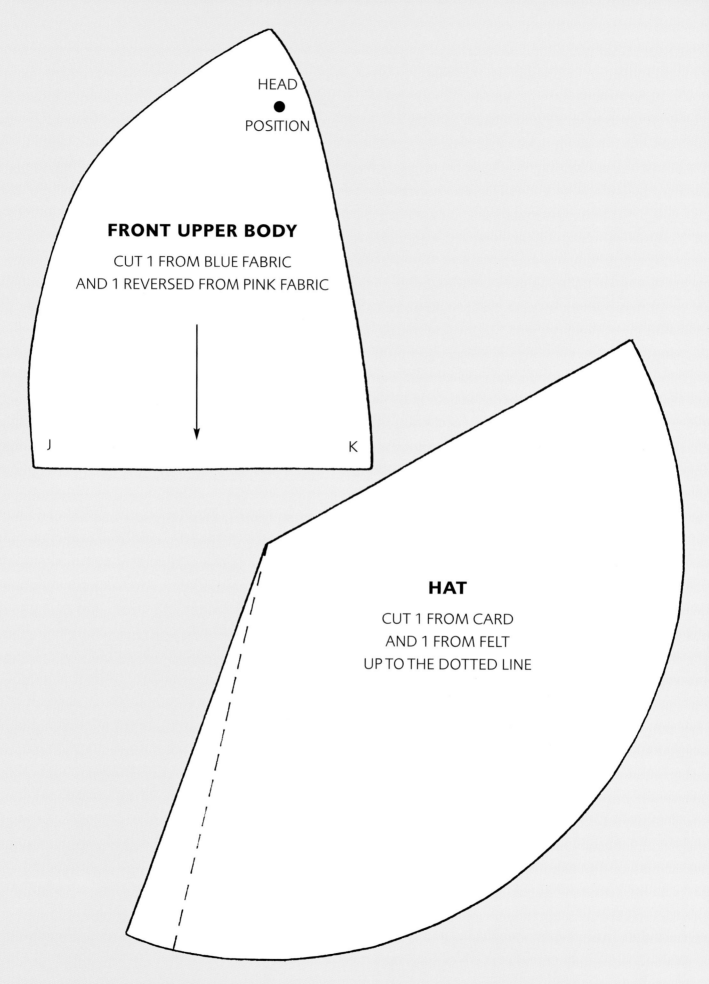

HEAD

POSITION

FRONT UPPER BODY

CUT 1 FROM BLUE FABRIC
AND 1 REVERSED FROM PINK FABRIC

J

K

HAT

CUT 1 FROM CARD
AND 1 FROM FELT
UP TO THE DOTTED LINE

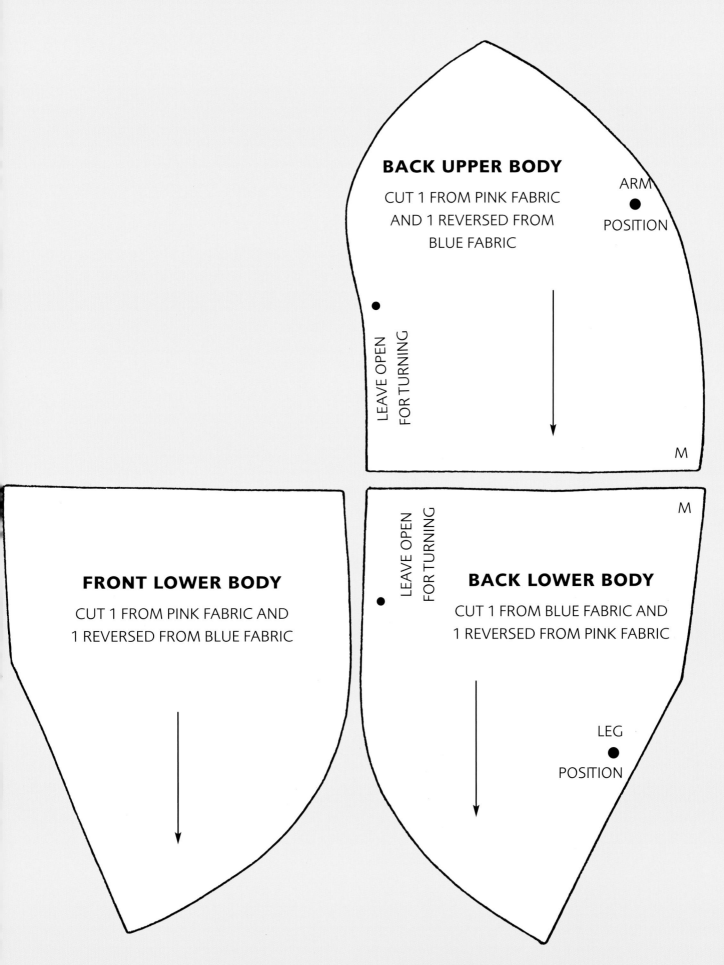

BACK UPPER BODY

CUT 1 FROM PINK FABRIC
AND 1 REVERSED FROM
BLUE FABRIC

ARM
POSITION

LEAVE OPEN FOR TURNING

M

FRONT LOWER BODY

CUT 1 FROM PINK FABRIC AND
1 REVERSED FROM BLUE FABRIC

M

LEAVE OPEN FOR TURNING

BACK LOWER BODY

CUT 1 FROM BLUE FABRIC AND
1 REVERSED FROM PINK FABRIC

LEG
POSITION

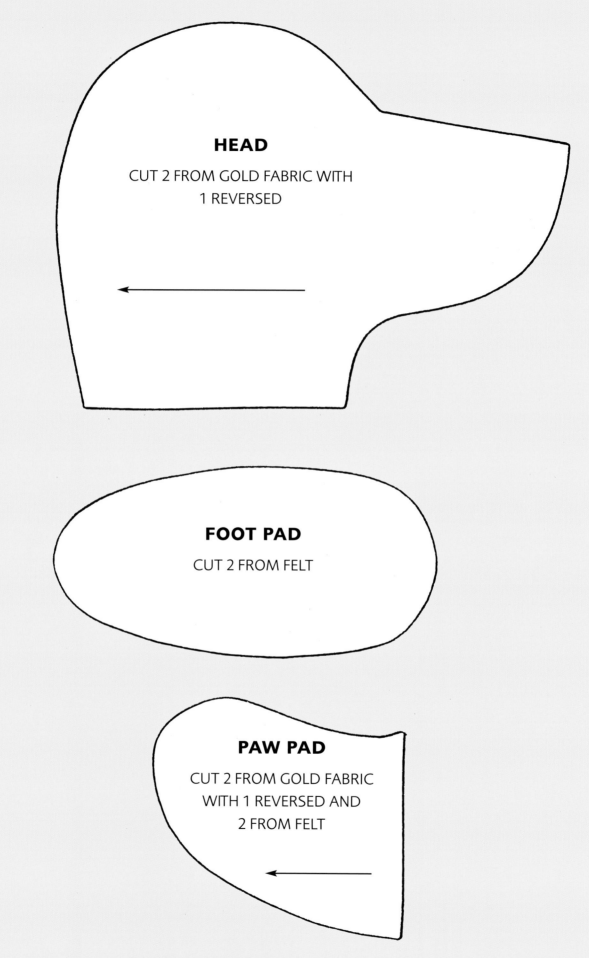

HEAD

CUT 2 FROM GOLD FABRIC WITH
1 REVERSED

FOOT PAD

CUT 2 FROM FELT

PAW PAD

CUT 2 FROM GOLD FABRIC
WITH 1 REVERSED AND
2 FROM FELT

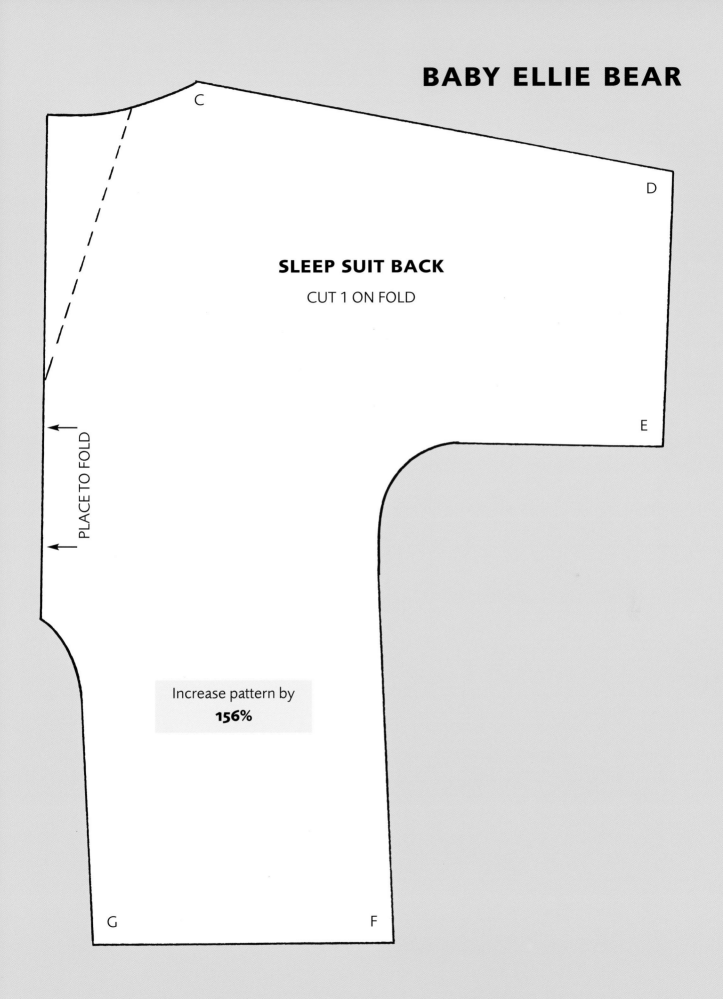

C

D

E

SLEEP SUIT BACK

CUT 1 ON FOLD

PLACE TO FOLD

Increase pattern by
156%

G

F

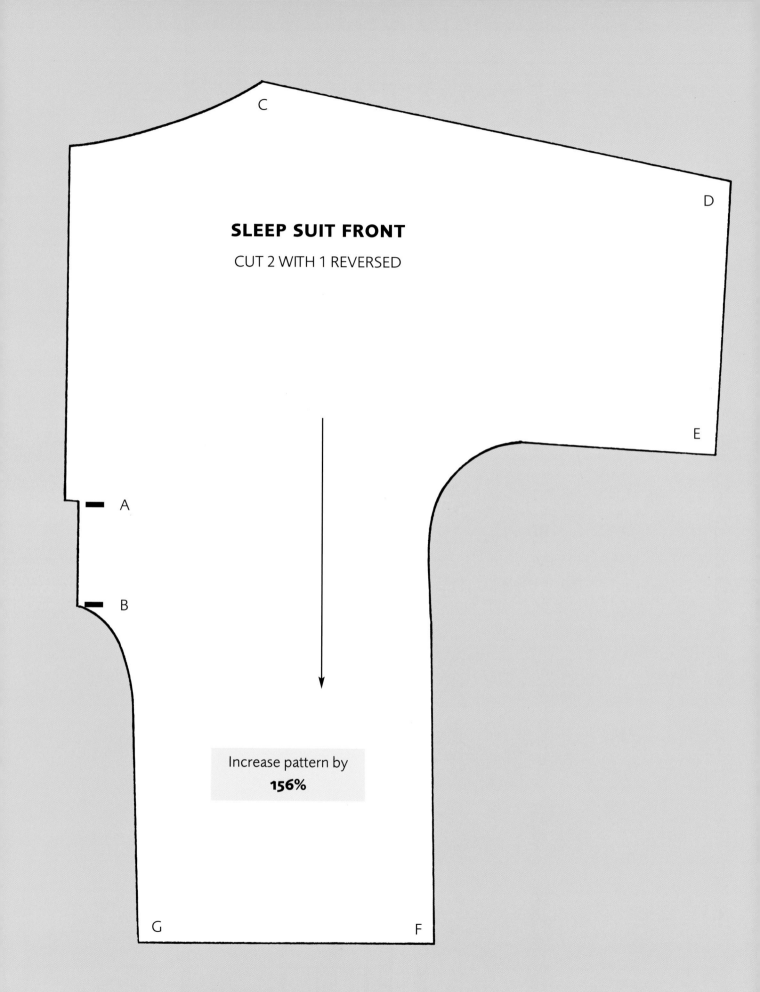

SLEEP SUIT FRONT

CUT 2 WITH 1 REVERSED

Increase pattern by
156%

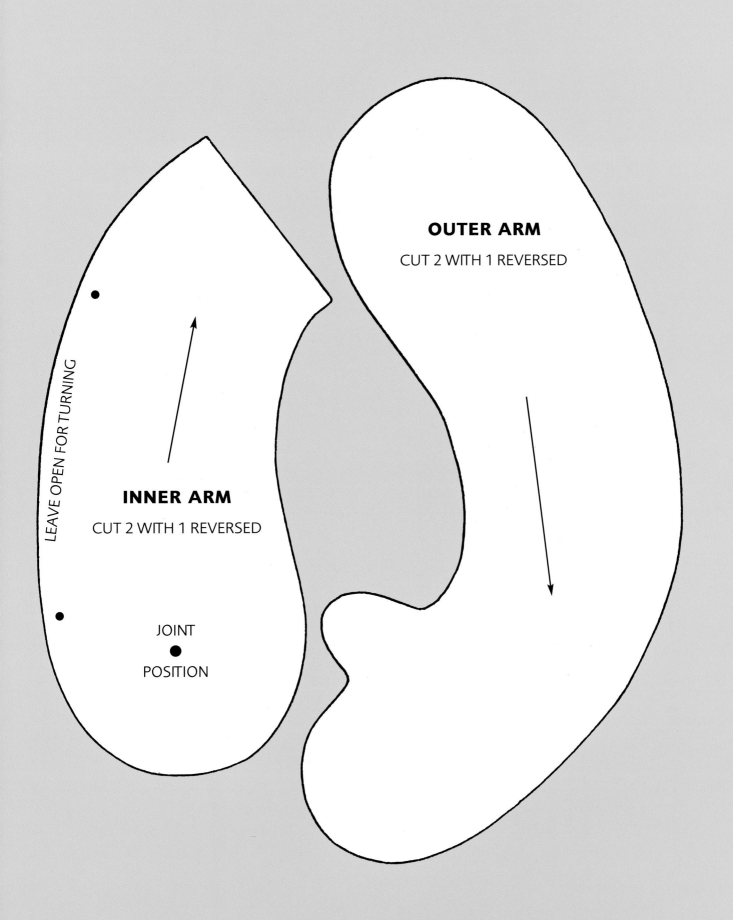

LEAVE OPEN FOR TURNING

INNER ARM

CUT 2 WITH 1 REVERSED

JOINT

POSITION

OUTER ARM

CUT 2 WITH 1 REVERSED

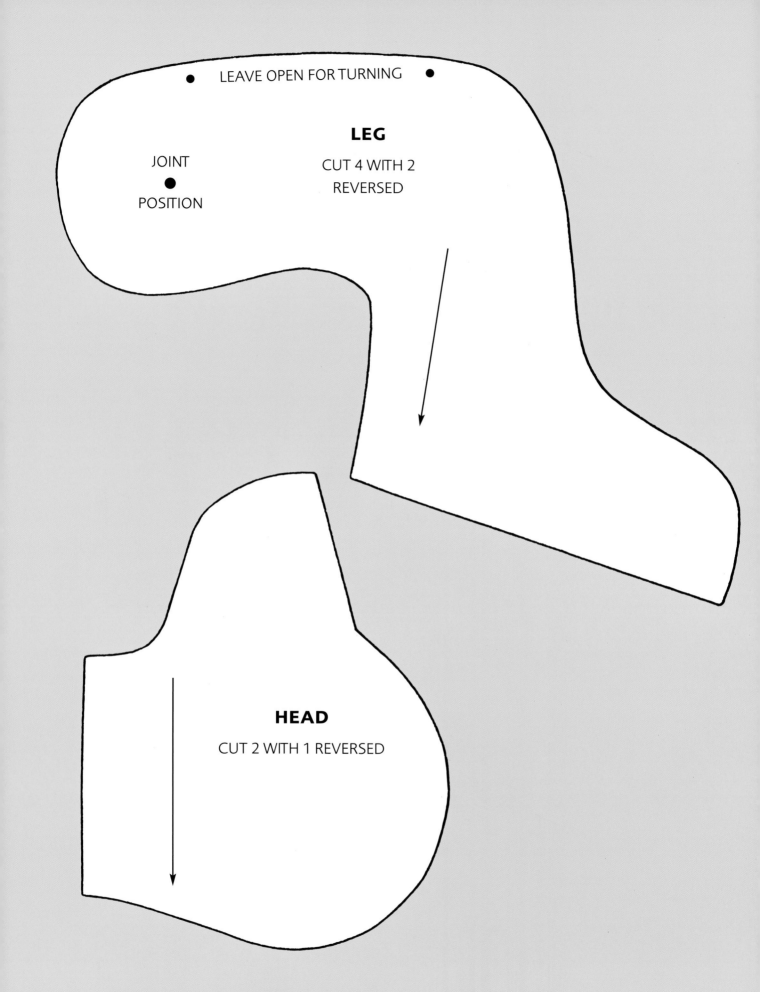

LEAVE OPEN FOR TURNING

LEG

JOINT

CUT 4 WITH 2
REVERSED

POSITION

HEAD

CUT 2 WITH 1 REVERSED

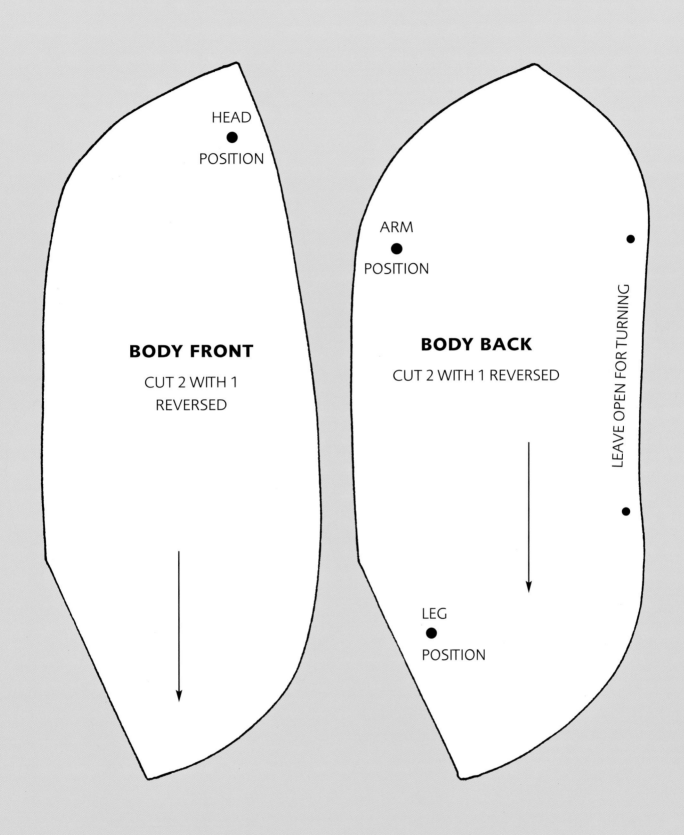

HEAD

POSITION

ARM

POSITION

LEAVE OPEN FOR TURNING

BODY FRONT

CUT 2 WITH 1
REVERSED

BODY BACK

CUT 2 WITH 1 REVERSED

LEG

POSITION

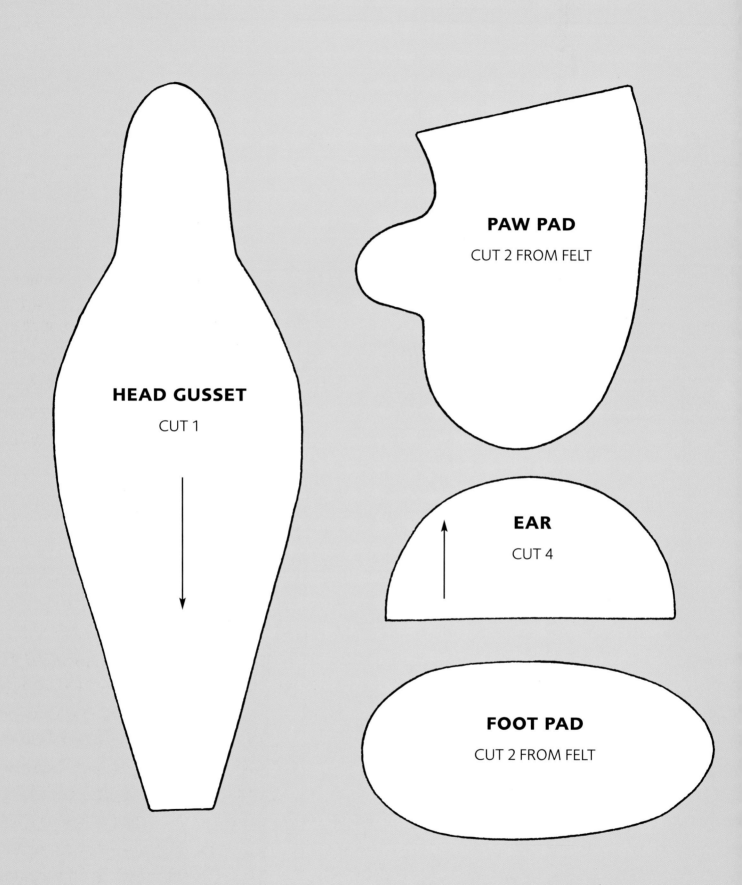

HEAD GUSSET

CUT 1

PAW PAD

CUT 2 FROM FELT

EAR

CUT 4

FOOT PAD

CUT 2 FROM FELT

EMBROIDERED BEARS

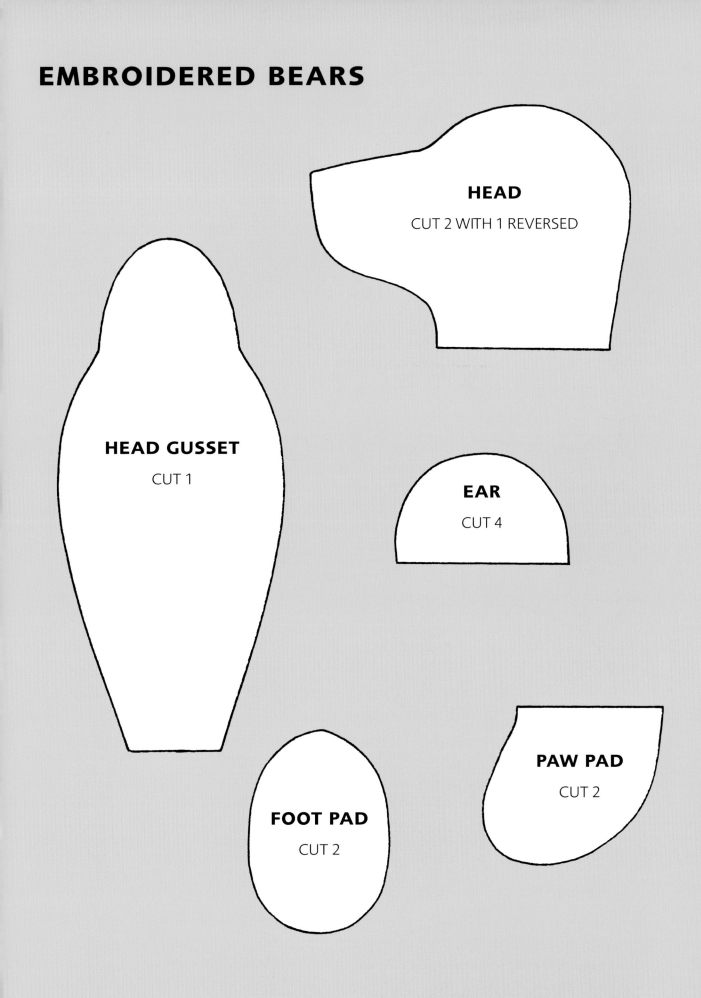

HEAD

CUT 2 WITH 1 REVERSED

HEAD GUSSET

CUT 1

EAR

CUT 4

PAW PAD

CUT 2

FOOT PAD

CUT 2

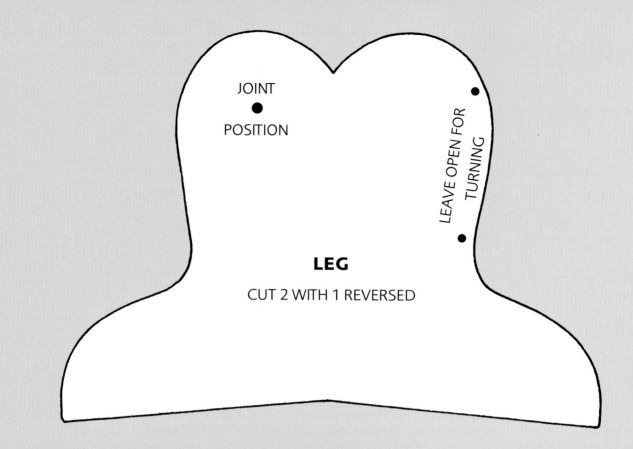

LEG

CUT 2 WITH 1 REVERSED

JOINT
POSITION

LEAVE OPEN FOR TURNING

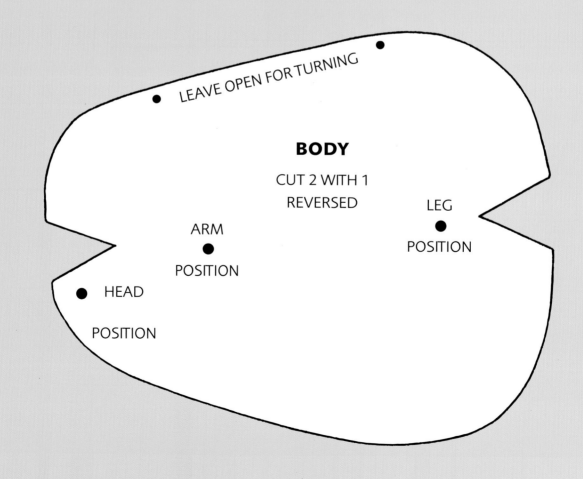

LEAVE OPEN FOR TURNING

BODY

CUT 2 WITH 1
REVERSED

ARM
POSITION

LEG
POSITION

HEAD

POSITION

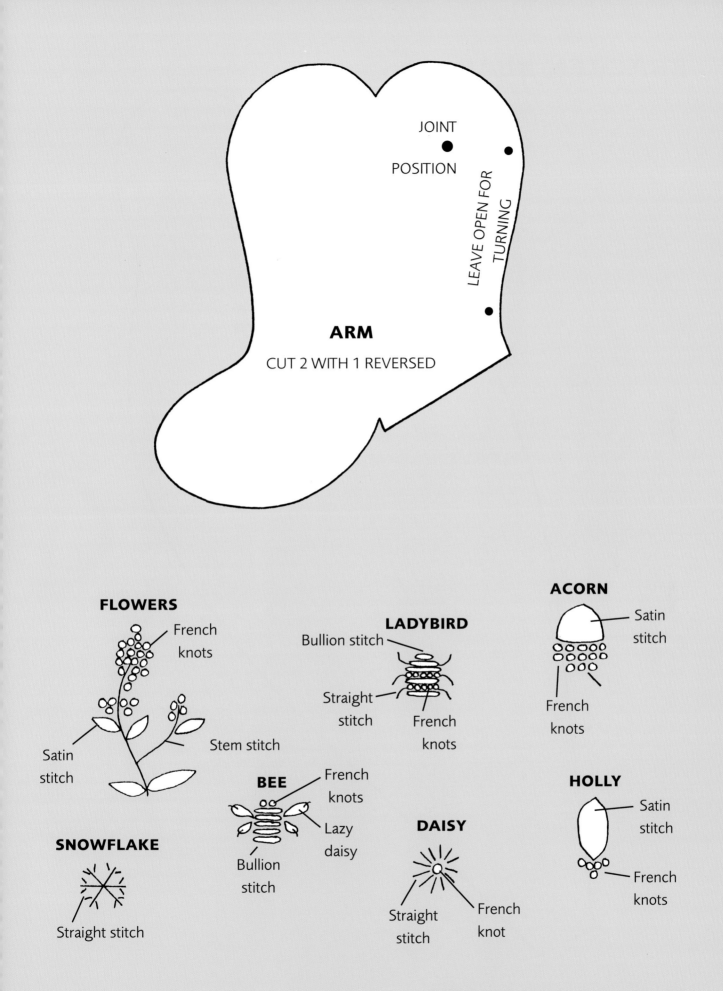

JOINT

POSITION

LEAVE OPEN FOR TURNING

ARM

CUT 2 WITH 1 REVERSED

FLOWERS

French knots

Satin stitch

Stem stitch

SNOWFLAKE

Straight stitch

BEE

French knots

Lazy daisy

Bullion stitch

LADYBIRD

Bullion stitch

Straight stitch

French knots

DAISY

Straight stitch

French knot

ACORN

Satin stitch

French knots

HOLLY

Satin stitch

French knots

BRACKEN BEAR

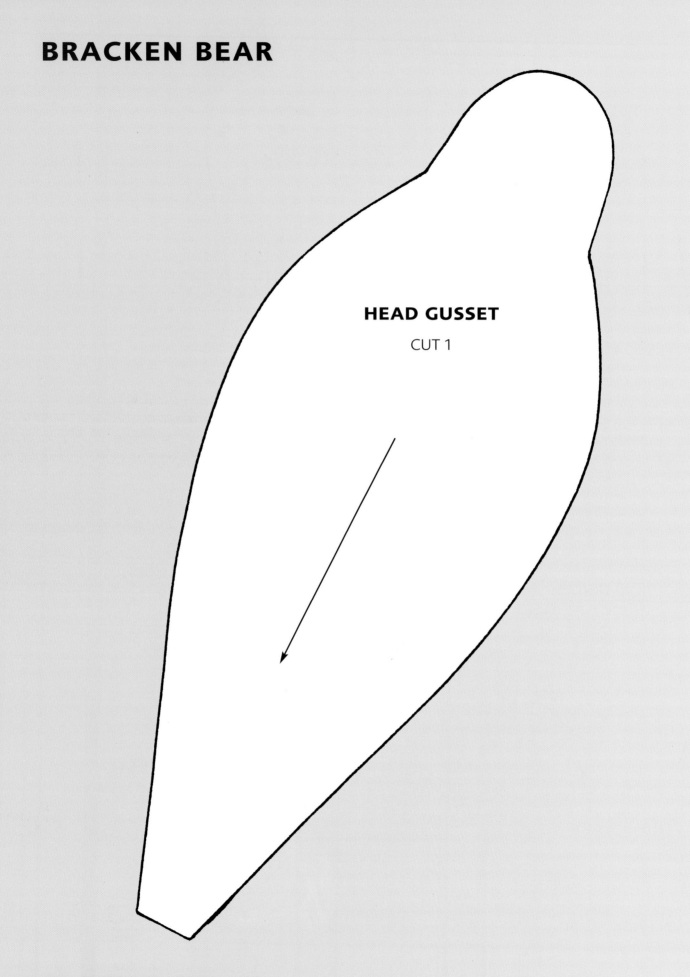

HEAD GUSSET

CUT 1

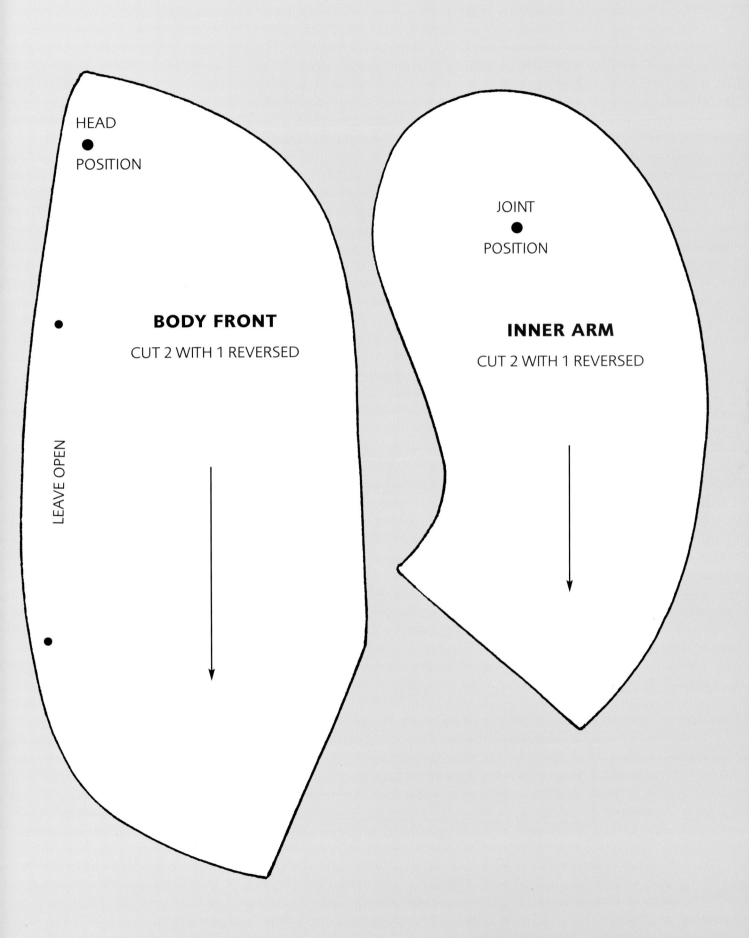

HEAD

POSITION

BODY FRONT

CUT 2 WITH 1 REVERSED

LEAVE OPEN

JOINT

POSITION

INNER ARM

CUT 2 WITH 1 REVERSED

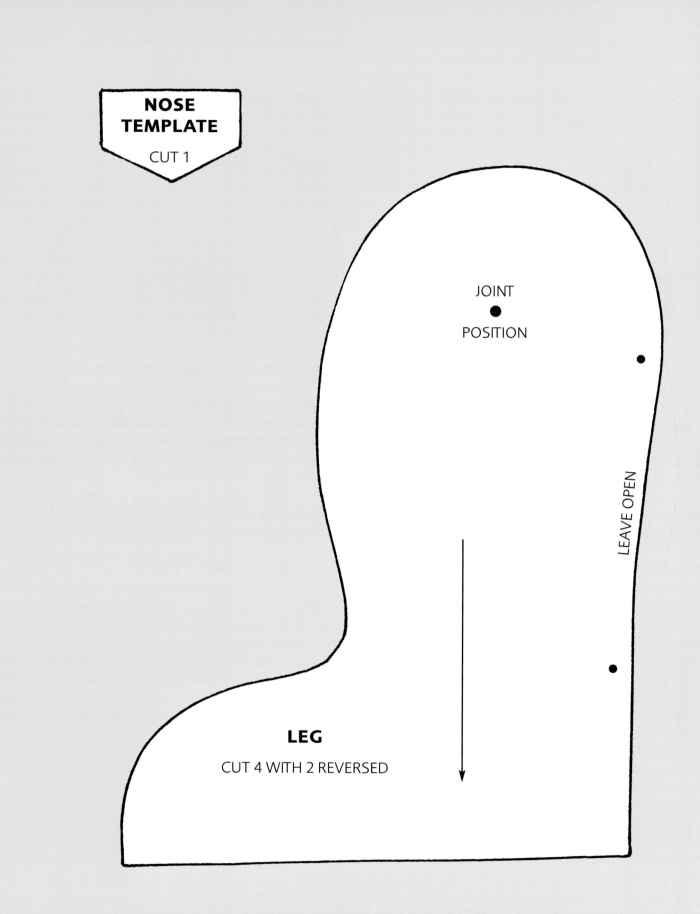

NOSE TEMPLATE

CUT 1

JOINT

POSITION

LEAVE OPEN

LEG

CUT 4 WITH 2 REVERSED

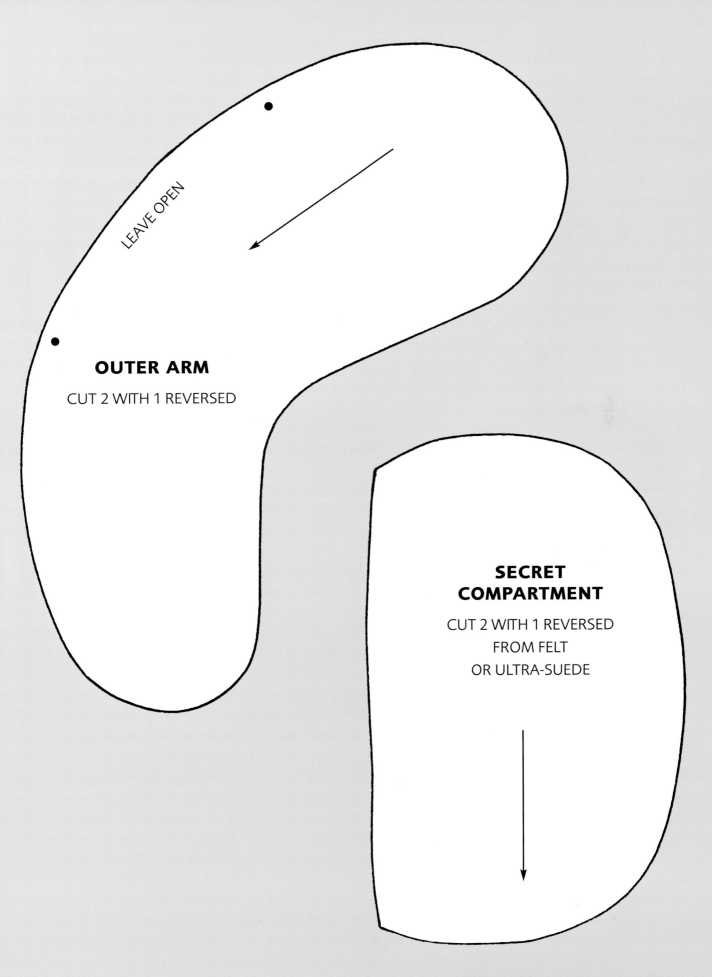

LEAVE OPEN

OUTER ARM

CUT 2 WITH 1 REVERSED

SECRET COMPARTMENT

CUT 2 WITH 1 REVERSED
FROM FELT
OR ULTRA-SUEDE

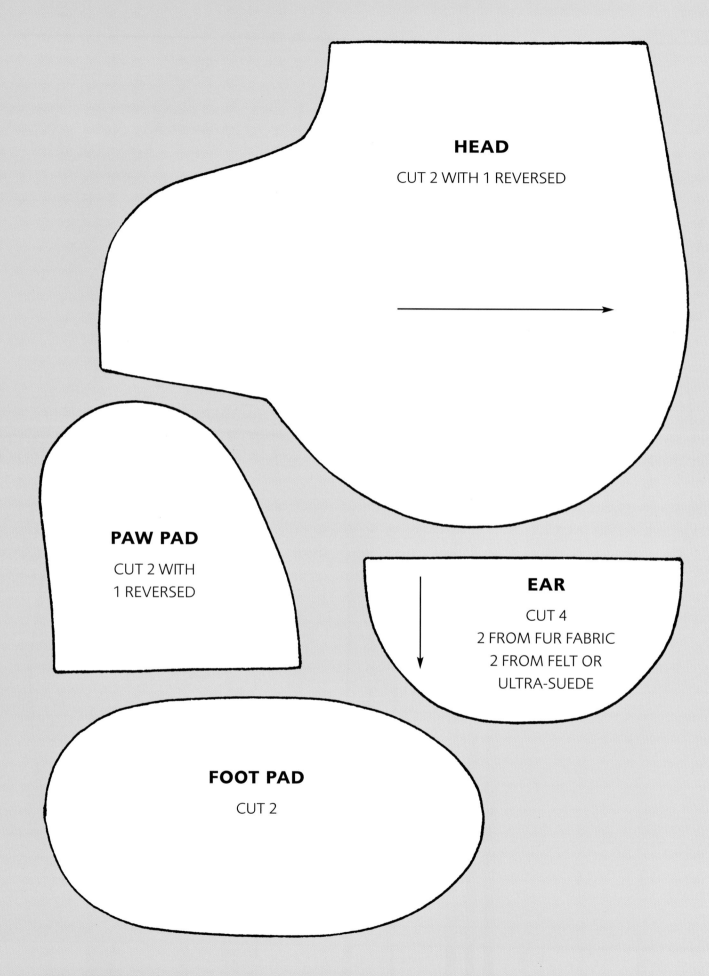

HEAD

CUT 2 WITH 1 REVERSED

PAW PAD

CUT 2 WITH
1 REVERSED

EAR

CUT 4
2 FROM FUR FABRIC
2 FROM FELT OR
ULTRA-SUEDE

FOOT PAD

CUT 2

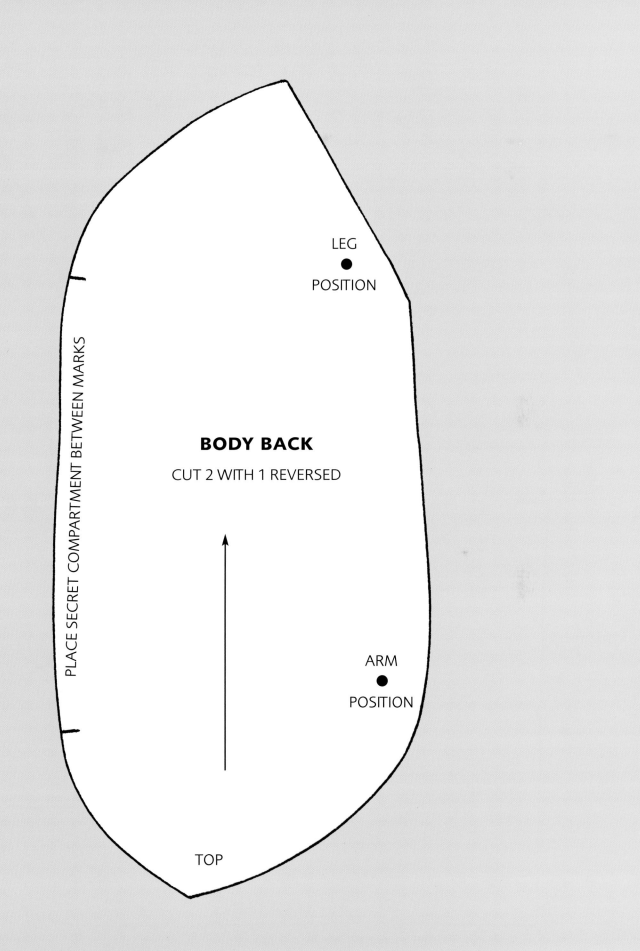

LEG

● POSITION

BODY BACK

CUT 2 WITH 1 REVERSED

PLACE SECRET COMPARTMENT BETWEEN MARKS

ARM

● POSITION

TOP

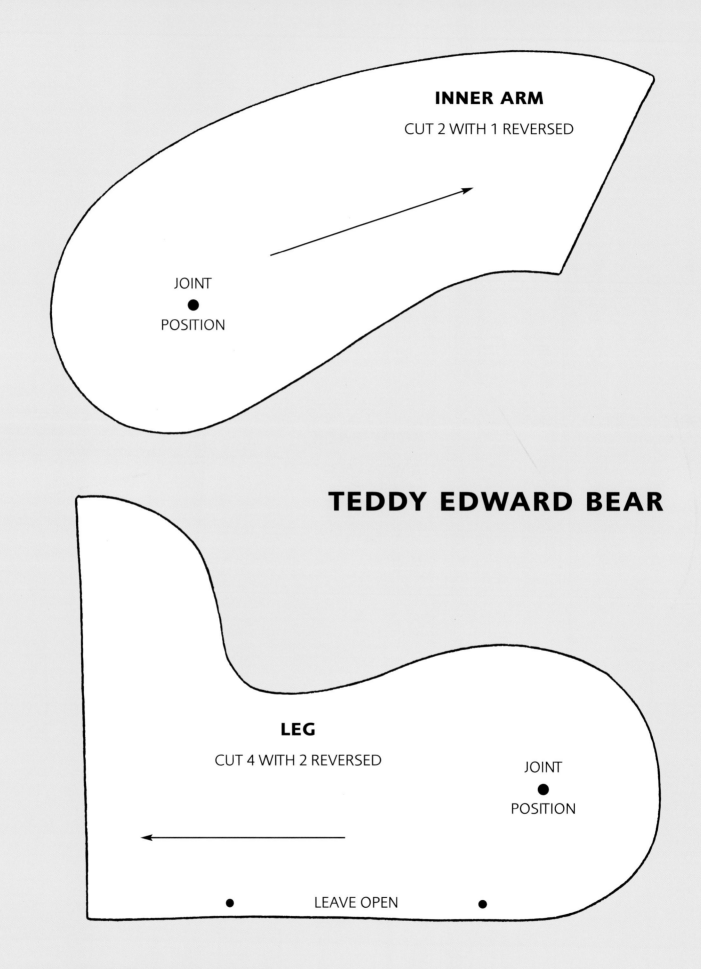

INNER ARM

CUT 2 WITH 1 REVERSED

JOINT

●

POSITION

TEDDY EDWARD BEAR

LEG

CUT 4 WITH 2 REVERSED

JOINT

●

POSITION

LEAVE OPEN

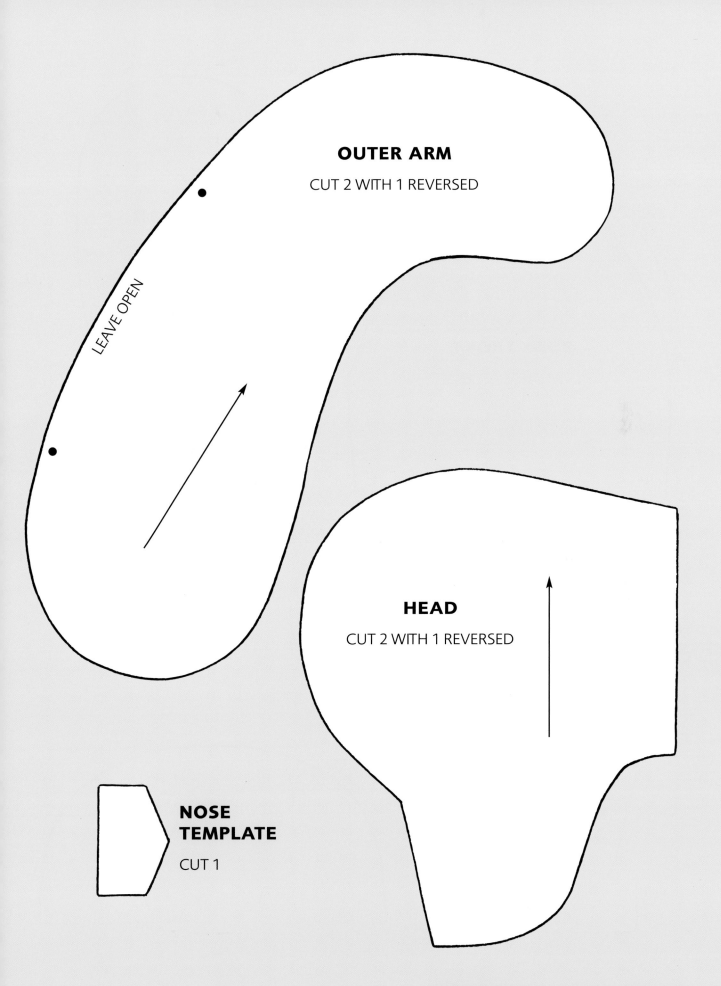

OUTER ARM

CUT 2 WITH 1 REVERSED

LEAVE OPEN

HEAD

CUT 2 WITH 1 REVERSED

NOSE TEMPLATE

CUT 1

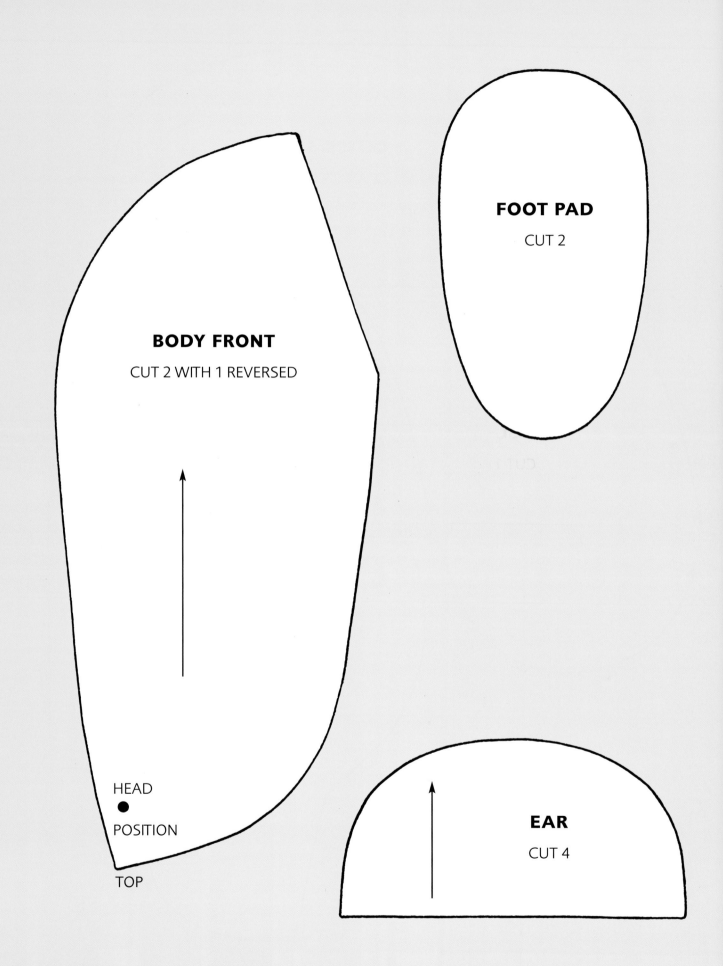

FOOT PAD

CUT 2

BODY FRONT

CUT 2 WITH 1 REVERSED

HEAD

●

POSITION

TOP

EAR

CUT 4

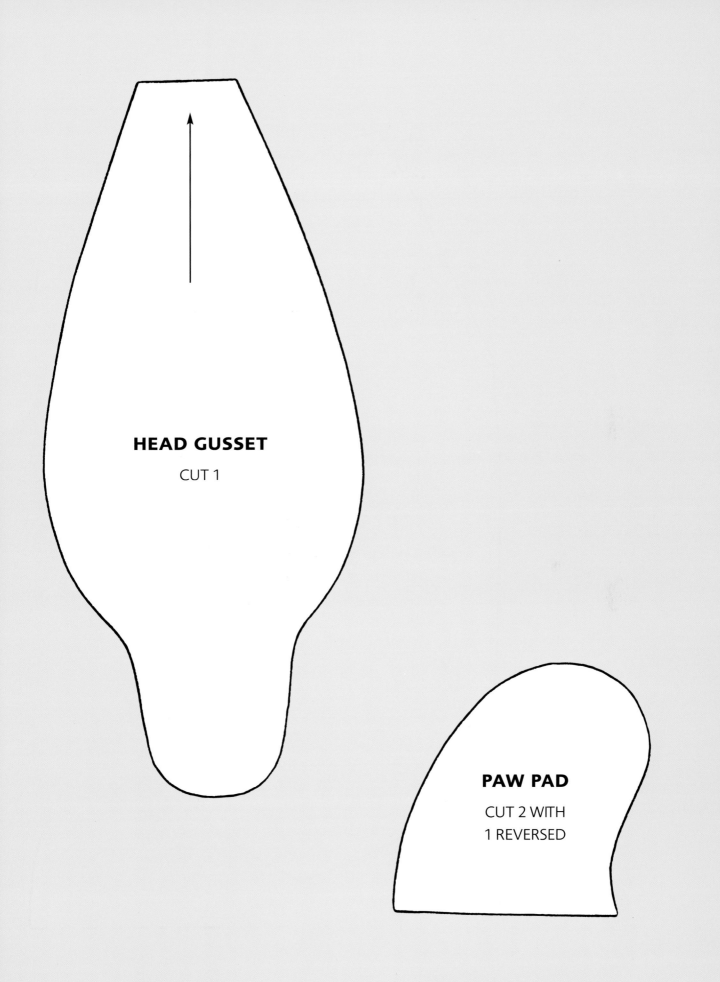

HEAD GUSSET

CUT 1

PAW PAD

CUT 2 WITH
1 REVERSED

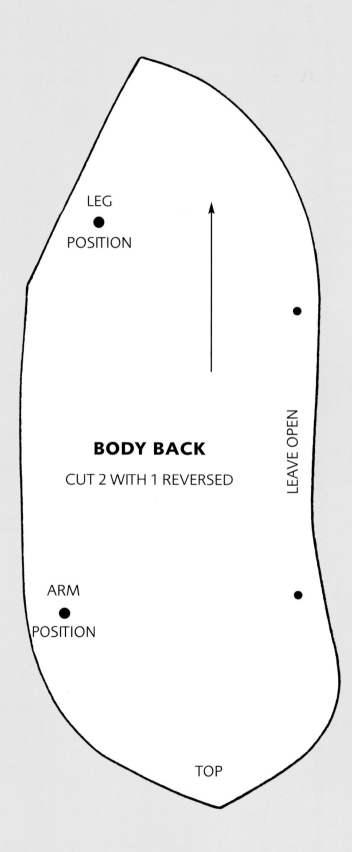

LEG

POSITION

BODY BACK

CUT 2 WITH 1 REVERSED

LEAVE OPEN

ARM

POSITION

TOP

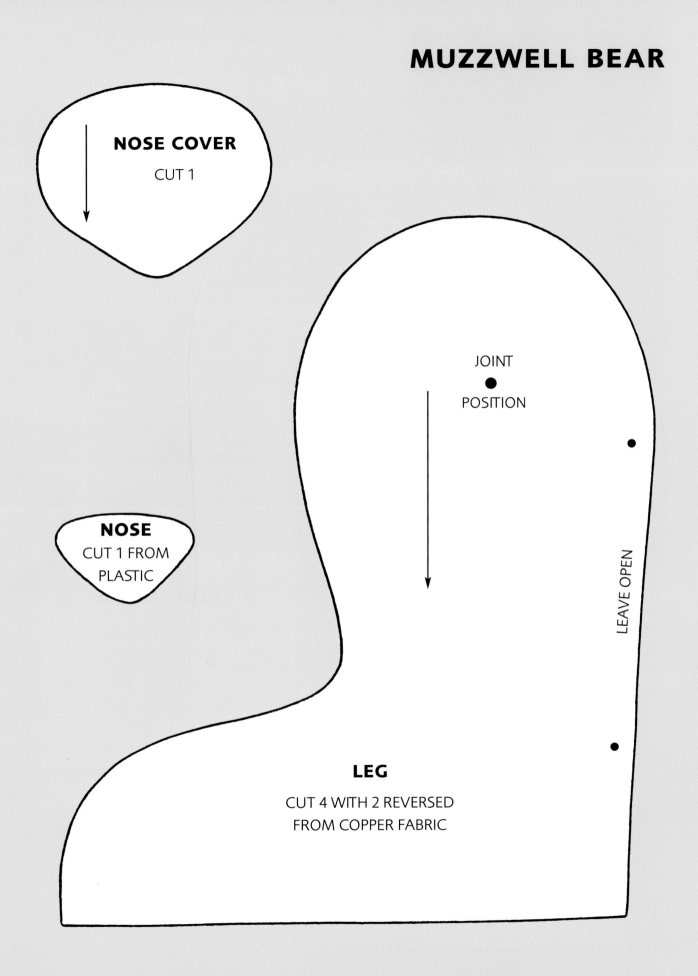

NOSE COVER

CUT 1

NOSE

CUT 1 FROM

PLASTIC

JOINT

POSITION

LEAVE OPEN

LEG

CUT 4 WITH 2 REVERSED

FROM COPPER FABRIC

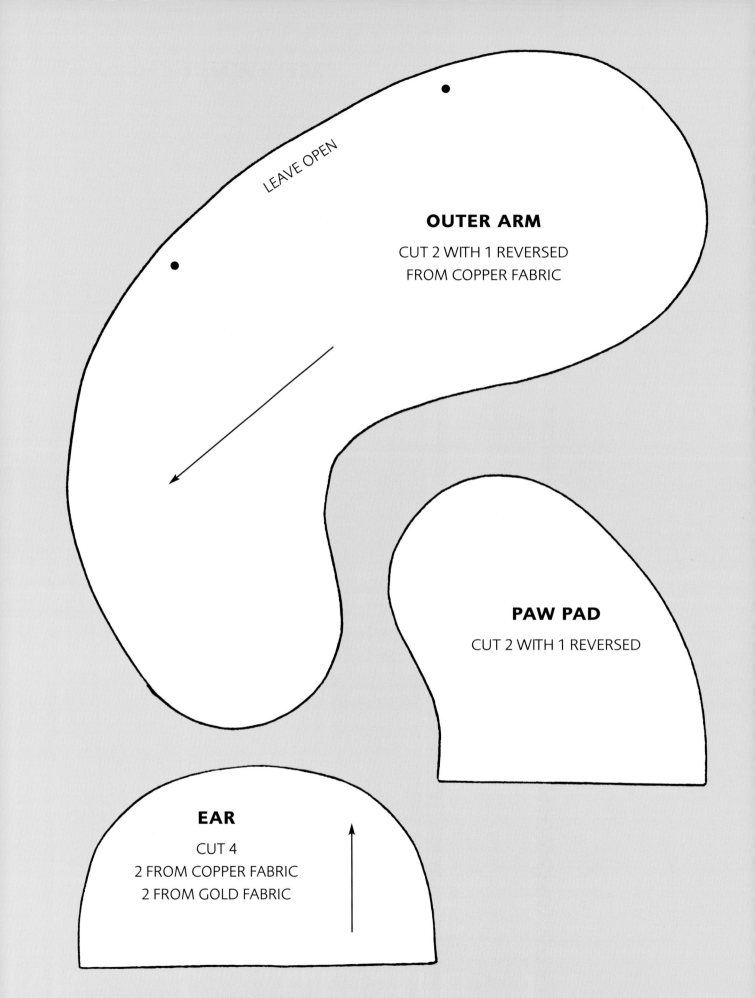

LEAVE OPEN

OUTER ARM

CUT 2 WITH 1 REVERSED
FROM COPPER FABRIC

PAW PAD

CUT 2 WITH 1 REVERSED

EAR

CUT 4
2 FROM COPPER FABRIC
2 FROM GOLD FABRIC

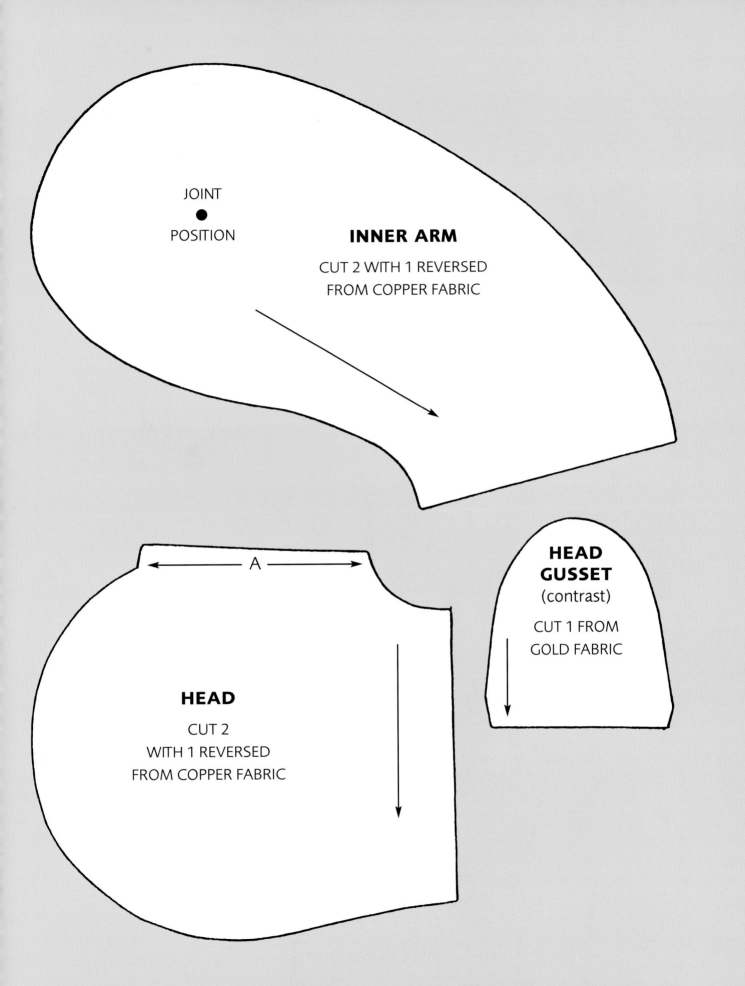

JOINT
●
POSITION

INNER ARM

CUT 2 WITH 1 REVERSED
FROM COPPER FABRIC

HEAD GUSSET
(contrast)

CUT 1 FROM
GOLD FABRIC

A

HEAD

CUT 2
WITH 1 REVERSED
FROM COPPER FABRIC

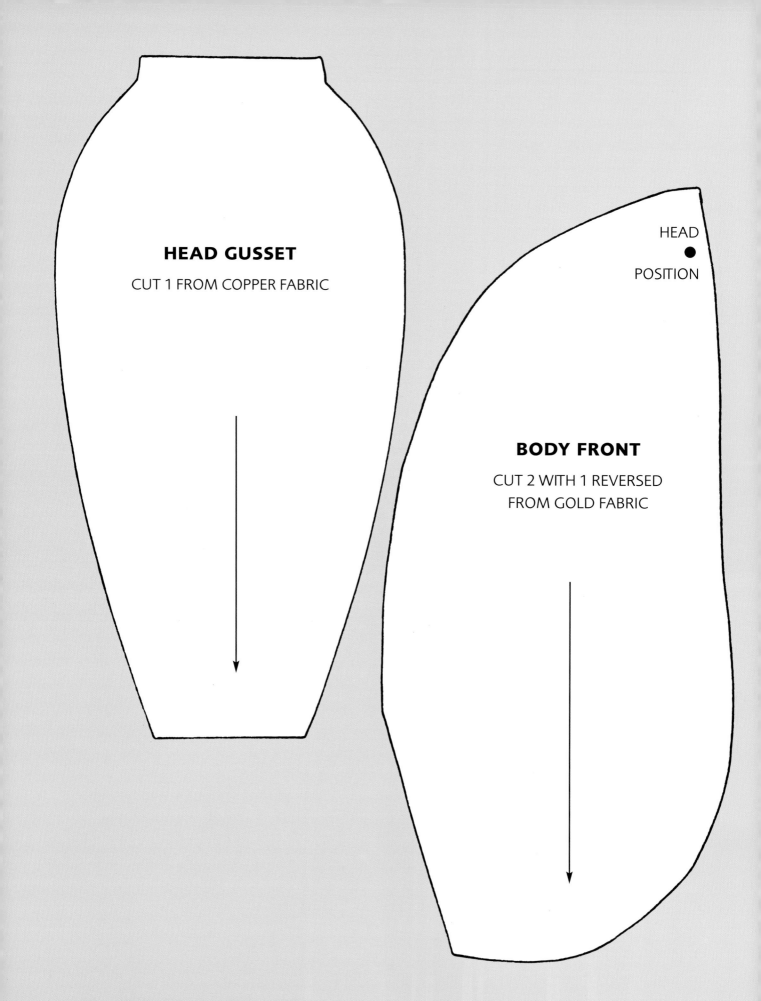

HEAD GUSSET

CUT 1 FROM COPPER FABRIC

HEAD

● POSITION

BODY FRONT

CUT 2 WITH 1 REVERSED
FROM GOLD FABRIC

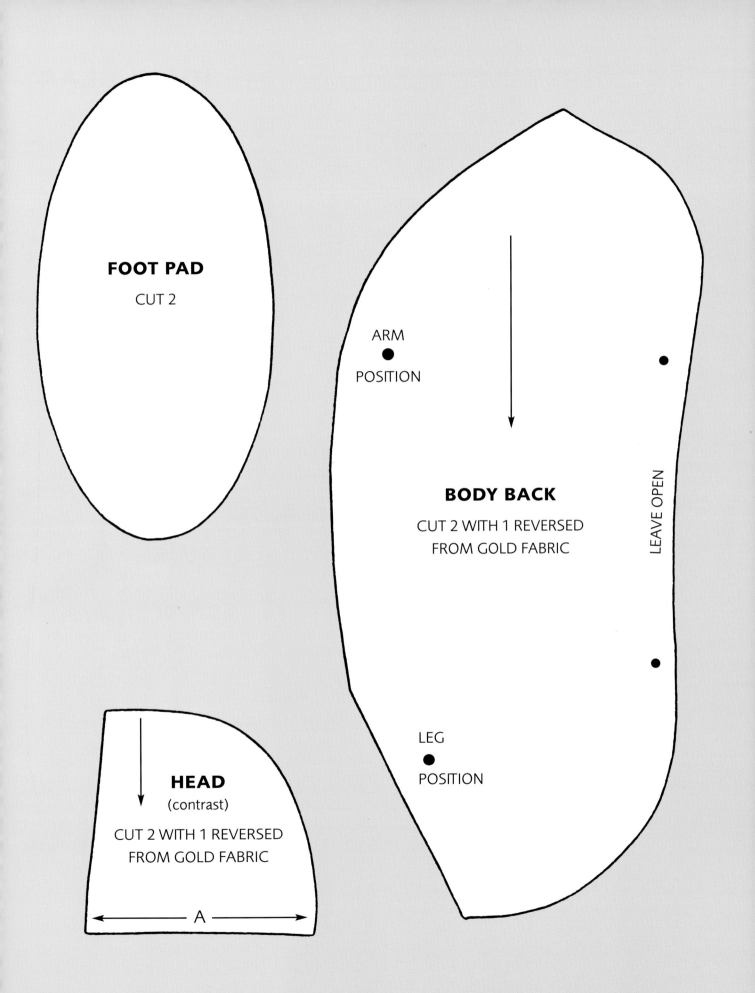

FOOT PAD

CUT 2

ARM
●
POSITION

LEAVE OPEN

BODY BACK

CUT 2 WITH 1 REVERSED
FROM GOLD FABRIC

LEG
●
POSITION

HEAD
(contrast)

CUT 2 WITH 1 REVERSED
FROM GOLD FABRIC

←——— A ———→

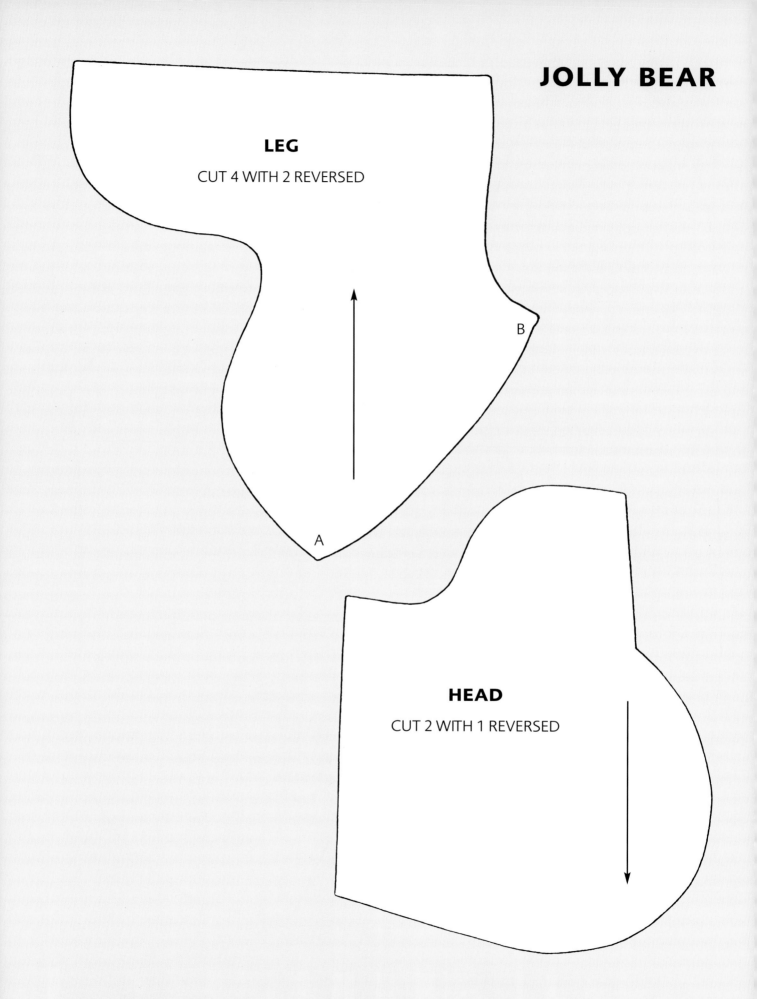

JOLLY BEAR

LEG

CUT 4 WITH 2 REVERSED

B

A

HEAD

CUT 2 WITH 1 REVERSED

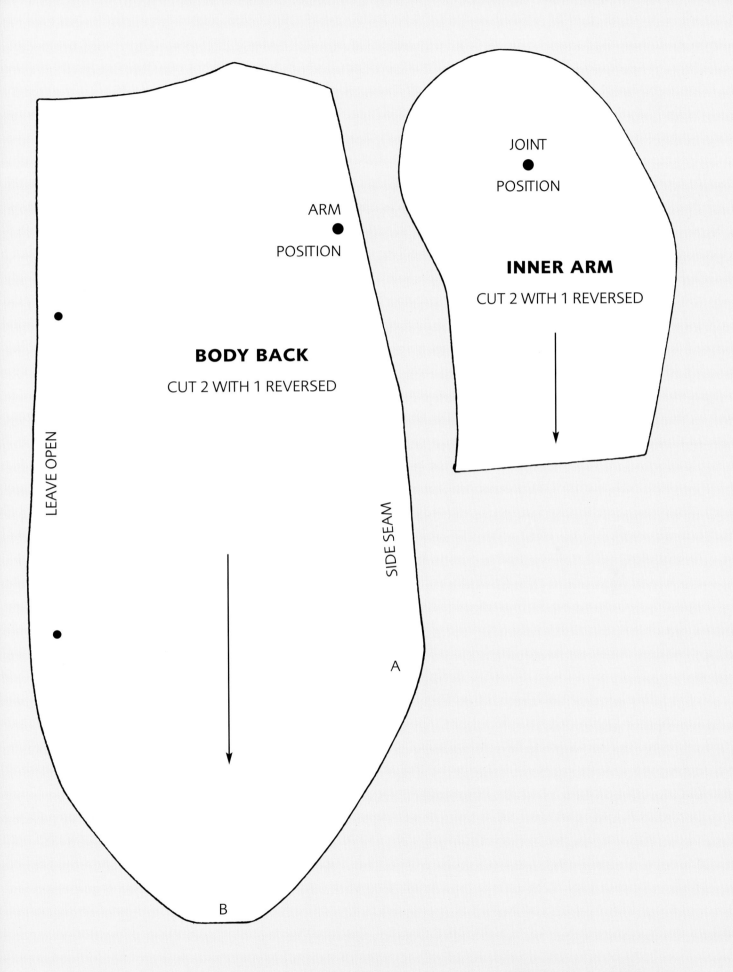

ARM

● POSITION

JOINT

● POSITION

INNER ARM

CUT 2 WITH 1 REVERSED

BODY BACK

CUT 2 WITH 1 REVERSED

LEAVE OPEN

SIDE SEAM

A

B

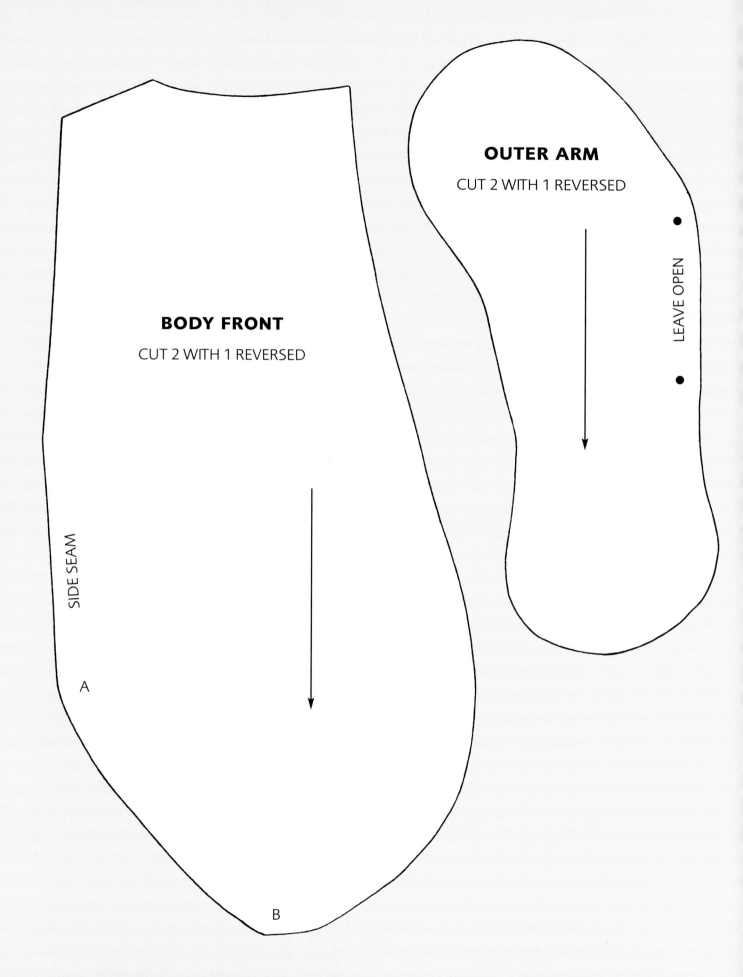

OUTER ARM

CUT 2 WITH 1 REVERSED

LEAVE OPEN

BODY FRONT

CUT 2 WITH 1 REVERSED

SIDE SEAM

A

B

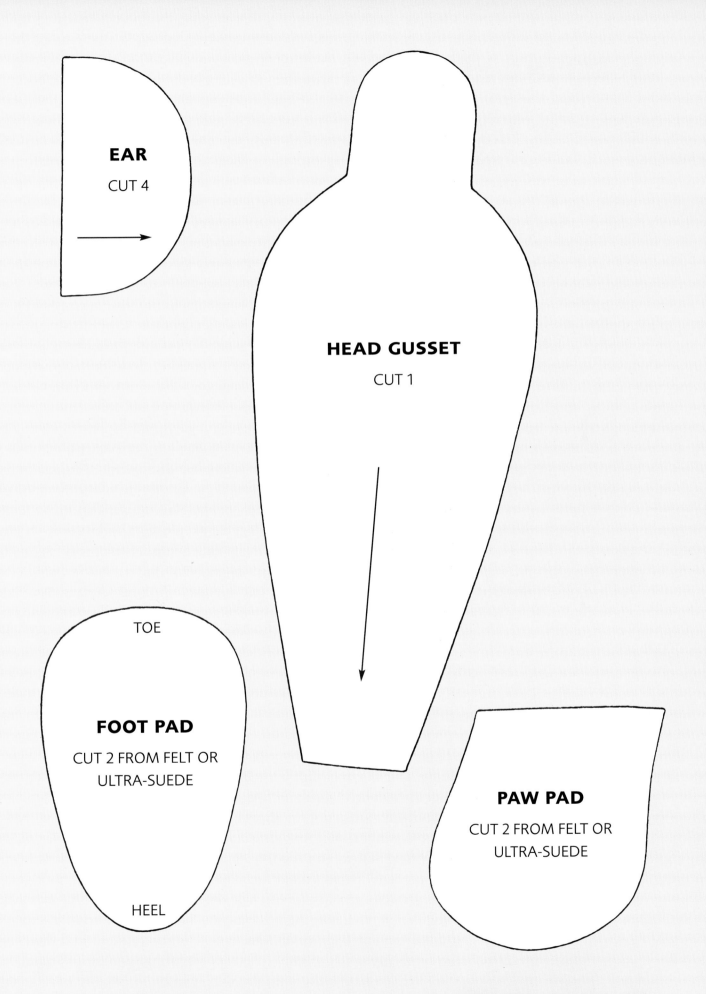

EAR

CUT 4

HEAD GUSSET

CUT 1

TOE

FOOT PAD

CUT 2 FROM FELT OR
ULTRA-SUEDE

HEEL

PAW PAD

CUT 2 FROM FELT OR
ULTRA-SUEDE

SLEEPING BEAR

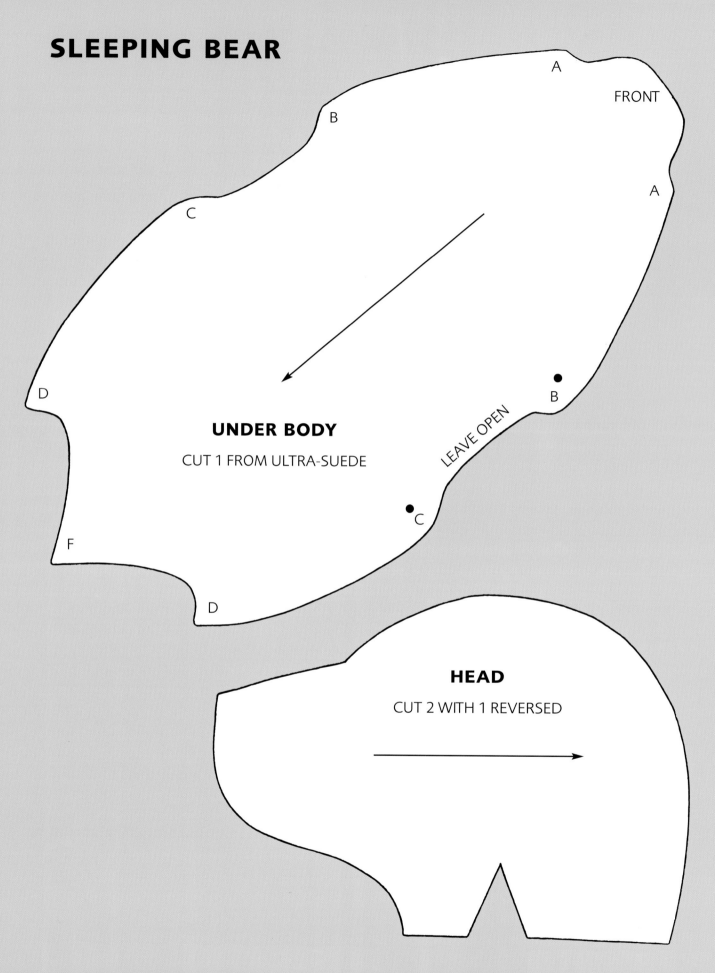

A

FRONT

B

A

C

UNDER BODY

CUT 1 FROM ULTRA-SUEDE

D

LEAVE OPEN

B

C

F

D

HEAD

CUT 2 WITH 1 REVERSED

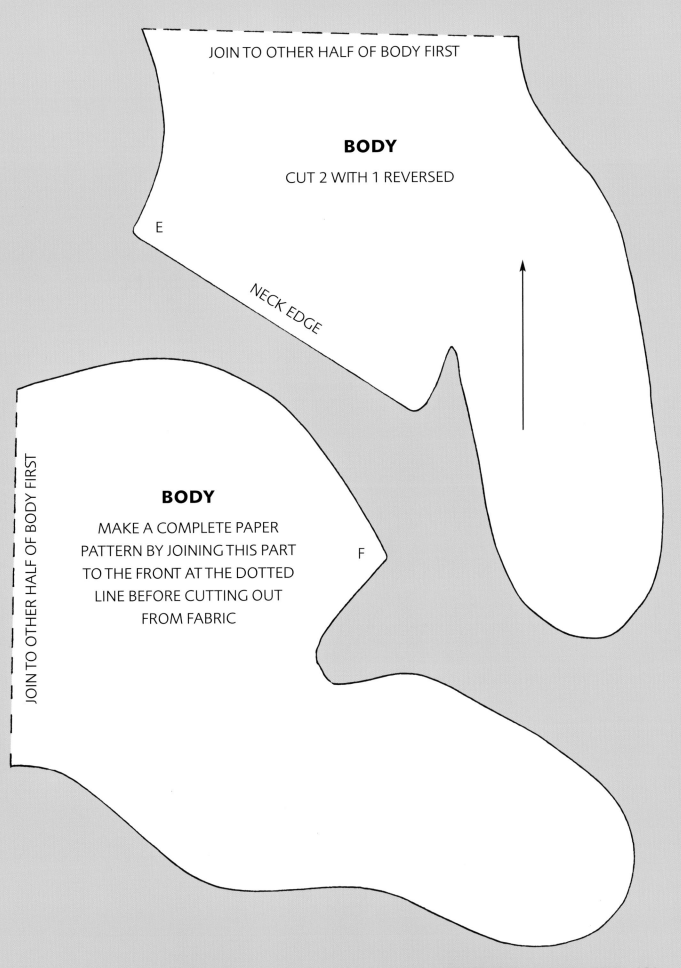

JOIN TO OTHER HALF OF BODY FIRST

BODY

CUT 2 WITH 1 REVERSED

E

NECK EDGE

BODY

MAKE A COMPLETE PAPER
PATTERN BY JOINING THIS PART
TO THE FRONT AT THE DOTTED
LINE BEFORE CUTTING OUT
FROM FABRIC

F

JOIN TO OTHER HALF OF BODY FIRST

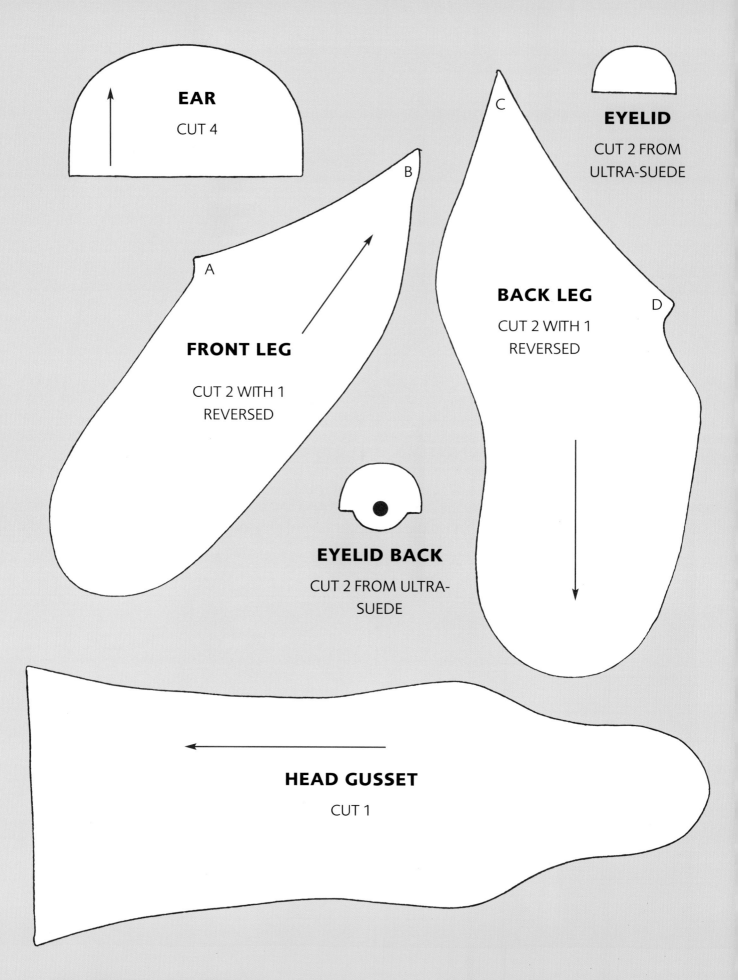

EAR

CUT 4

EYELID

CUT 2 FROM
ULTRA-SUEDE

B

A

FRONT LEG

CUT 2 WITH 1
REVERSED

C

BACK LEG

CUT 2 WITH 1
REVERSED

D

EYELID BACK

CUT 2 FROM ULTRA-
SUEDE

HEAD GUSSET

CUT 1

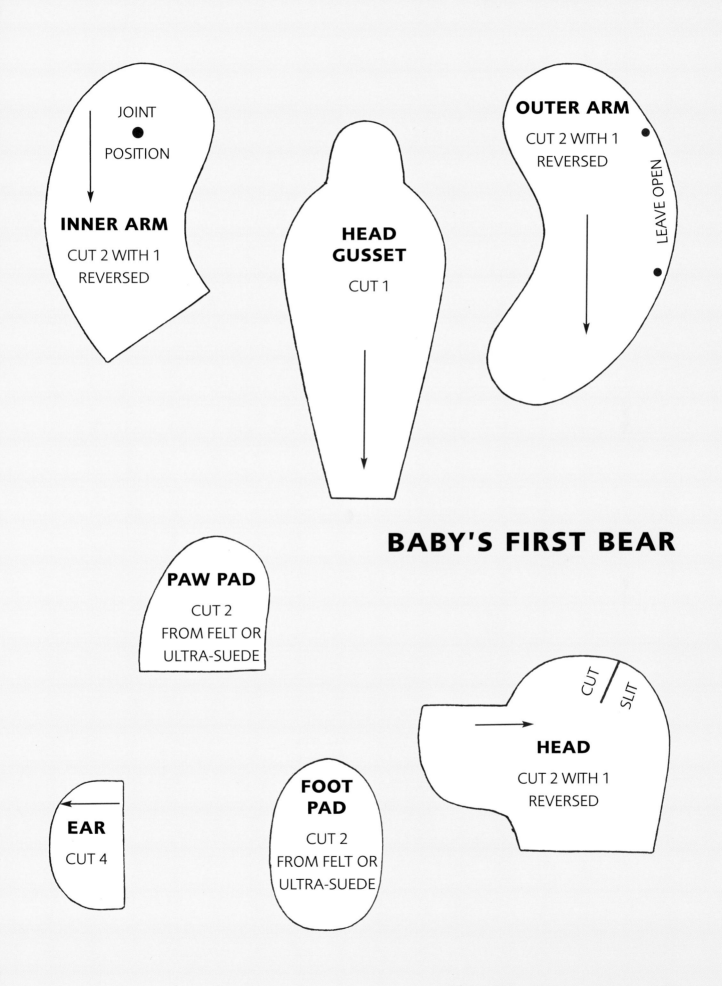

JOINT
POSITION

INNER ARM

CUT 2 WITH 1
REVERSED

**HEAD
GUSSET**

CUT 1

OUTER ARM

CUT 2 WITH 1
REVERSED

LEAVE OPEN

BABY'S FIRST BEAR

PAW PAD

CUT 2
FROM FELT OR
ULTRA-SUEDE

CUT

SLIT

HEAD

CUT 2 WITH 1
REVERSED

EAR

CUT 4

**FOOT
PAD**

CUT 2
FROM FELT OR
ULTRA-SUEDE

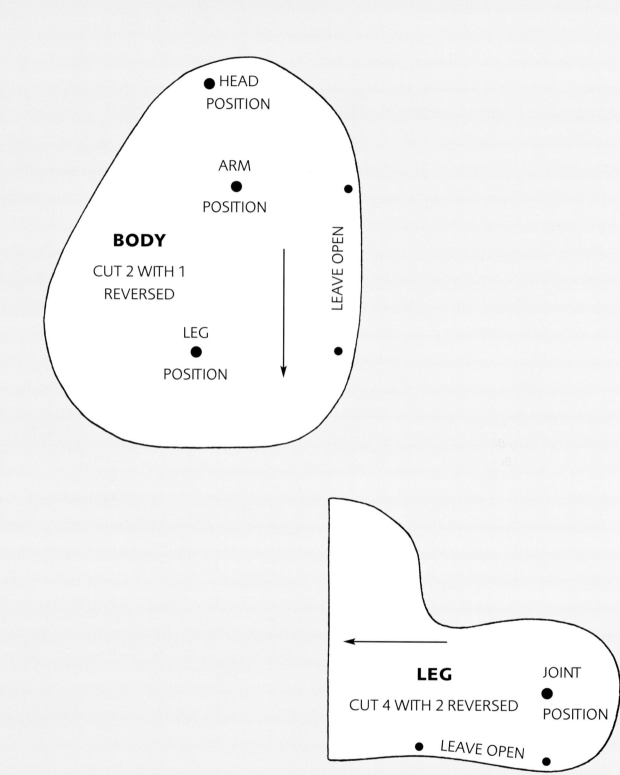

● HEAD
POSITION

ARM
● POSITION

BODY

CUT 2 WITH 1
REVERSED

LEAVE OPEN

LEG
● POSITION

LEG

CUT 4 WITH 2 REVERSED

JOINT
● POSITION

● LEAVE OPEN

SUPPLIERS

We recommend before requesting information from a mail order supplier, you contact them first as there is usually a small charge for catalogues and samples.

Brian and Donna Gibbs – Bridon Bears
Bears Cottage, 42 St Michael's Lane, Bridport,
Dorset, DT6 3RD
Tel: (01308) 420796
Web: http://www.bridonbears.force9.co.uk
Suppliers of traditional bear kits and patterns, authors of *Making Traditional Teddy Bears*, *Making and Dressing Traditional Teddy Bears* and *Making Teddy Bears To Treasure*. Also regular contributors to magazines.

Teddy Bear Warehouse Ltd,
Unit 11, D2 Trading Estate, Castle Road, Sittingbourne,
Kent, ME10 3RH.
Tel: (01795) 478775 Fax: (01795) 474494
Suppliers of mohair fabric, traditional and safety components, fillings, patterns and kits, and many teddy bear accessories.
Supplied materials for the following bears: Barney, Muzzwell, Baby's first bear, Traditional Teddy Edward, Bracken, and Jolly.

Admiral Bear Supplies,
37 Warren Drive, Ruislip, Middlesex, HA4 9RD.
Tel/Fax: 0208 8689598
Suppliers of mohair and some synthetic fabrics, traditional and safety components, patterns and accessories.
Supplied materials for the following bears: Baby Ellie, Harley and Sleeping Bear.

Fred Aldous Ltd
37 Lever Street, Manchester, M1 1LW.
Tel 0161-236 2477 Fax: 0161-236 6075
Web: http://www.fredaldous.co.uk
Suppliers of all types of art and craft materials with an extensive range of over 10,000 products, including toymaking accessories.
Supplied materials for the Four Seasons Embroidered bears.

Edinburgh Imports Ltd,
POB 722 – Woodland Hills, California 91365-0722, USA
Web: http://edinburgh.com
Suppliers of mohair and synthetic fur fabrics, traditional and safety components, patterns and kits and many other bear-making accessories
A. Helmbold GmbH.
Pluschweberei und Faberei, D-98634 Oberweid,
Haupstrasse 44, Germany.
Tel: 036946-22009 Fax: 036946-22020
Manufacturer of toy plush made from mohair, wool, alpaca, cotton and artificial silk.

Berelijn
Voorstraat 269,
3311 EP Dordrecht,
The Netherlands
Tel: 31 78 6318028 Fax: 31 78 631 0498
Web: www.berelijn.com
Supplies mohair fabric and bear making accessories
Der Bär,
Peter Stock,
Haupstrasse 55,
40789 Monheim,
Germany
Fax: 2173-60218
e-mail: der-Baer.P.Stock@t-online.de
Suppliers of top quality English and German mohair fabric.

FURTHER READING

The following magazines and publications contain information dedicated to teddy bears.

Teddy Bear Club International Magazine,
Aceville Publications Ltd., Castle House, 97 High Street, Colchester, Essex. CO1 1TH
Tel: (01206) 505978
Web: www.teddybearmagazine.com

Teddy Bear Times Magazine
Avalon Court, Star Road, Partridge Green, West Sussex, RH13 8RY
Tel: (01403) 711511 Fax: (01403) 711521
Web: http://www.teddybeartimes.com

Teddy Bear Scene Magazine,
EMF Publishing, 5–7 Elm Park, Ferring, West Sussex, BN12 5LL.
Tel (01903) 244900 Fax: (01903) 506626

The UK Teddy Bear Guide,
Hugglets, PO Box 290, Brighton, BN2 1DR
Tel: (01273) 697974 Fax: (01273) 626255
Web: http://www.hugglets.co.uk

INDEX